SCIENCE OF THE GODS

SCIENCE OF THE GODS

Reconciling Mystery and Matter

DAVID ASH and PETER HEWITT

Gateway Books, Bath.

First published in 1990
by Gateway Books
The Hollies, Wellow,
Bath, BA2 8QJ

Cover photo by Maurice Nimmo
Cover design by Studio B of Bristol
Set in 10½ on 12 pt Sabon
by Character Graphics of Taunton
Printed and bound by Billings of Worcester

British Library Cataloguing in Publication Data:
Ash, David A. (David Andrew) *1948-*
Science of the gods.
1. Religion, related to science
I. Title II Hewitt, Peter *1948-*
215
ISBN 0 946551-62-6

Contents

Acknowledgements

Many people contributed to the creation of the book. We would like to express our particular thanks to Sally Cartwright and Charles Dawes, who first encouraged it into being; Jack Smith, who made possible the production of the first draft; Sir George Trevelyan, whose support and enthusiasm for the project never flagged; and Nigel Blair, who generously provided books from his unique library. Nigel's breadth of knowledge guided our research on several occasions, and our contact with his Wessex Research Group network was highly stimulating.

Several people read the book at early draft stages and for their suggestions we are most grateful. Among those we would particularly like to thank are: Edward and Sally Baldwin, Lynora Brooke, Bob Gilson, Mike and Didi Hall, Dr D. M. A. Leggett, Eric Moody, Tim Wallace Murphy, Clive Neel, Trevor Ravenscroft and Bob Rogers. It would me misleading to suggest that they were all in agreement with everything that they read, but their comments were very helpful.

Extracts from an earlier version of *Science of the Gods* appeared in *Beyond Science* in May 1986, and in *Wessex Research Group Broadsheet No.10*, and we are grateful to their respective editors, James Cox and Nigel Blair, for this support. The evolution of the ideas also benefited from the opportunity to lecture at conferences: for providing this type of forum we owe gratitude in particular to The Radionic Association, The Scientific and Medical Network, The Stjaernsund Foundation, the Swiss Parapsychological Association, and the Wrekin Trust.

For their various encouragement or practical help in other ways we would like to thank: Sheila Best, Graham Browne, Hilary Cassidy, Felicity Evans, Dr Paul Filmore, Anne and Brian Heyman, Beth Holman, Adrian Jackson, Peggy Mason, Anthea Morton-Saner, the Marquis of Northampton, Jack Smith, Dorothy Stewart, Gloria Stewart, Josephine Veltri, Eric Vesey, Anne Wilkinson – and Sue Robertson for the use of Ceilidh in Dittisham, which provided an ideal environment in which to prepare the final version.

Our special thanks to David's wife Anna for her love and support to us both, and for taking on the main burden of their six children for two years so that we could be free to work full-time on the book.

Figures and Illustrations

Prologue

Teachings I discovered in a battered old book retrieved from an attic gave me a key that could transform present scientific ideas and usher in a magical new view of reality. As a sixteen year old I was practising yoga and the musty tome I had unearthed was on yogi philosophy. Based on lessons given in America in 1904, the book presented ideas handed down from ancient times. The crucial idea in its pages which was to change my life forever was that *matter is formed out of vortices of energy*. In this teaching, yogi philosophers appeared to have anticipated Einstein in realising that matter is equivalent to energy. This insight was eventually to lead me to penetrate into the deepest mysteries not only of science but also of religion.

When I was a nineteen year old student at university the professor of my faculty complained that instead of conceiving and championing their own new theories students attended merely to soak up information for exams. I had to prove him wrong. I began to work in earnest on the vortex. I quickly found that it provided an amazingly simple answer to mysteries that had baffled both scientists and philosophers over the ages. I realised that I had stumbled on a key of immense importance. To my utter astonishment, there seemed to be no end to what this single idea would explain. I was able firstly to resolve many of the conundrums and paradoxes of physics and then to go on to build a bridge between science and the supernatural. A pattern of great unity was unfolding.

It was as if I was placing piece after piece into an extraordinary jigsaw puzzle. It took me many years to complete but then, standing back to admire the work, I found myself looking on a completely new panorama of the universe.

As a child, my father taught me to question in the manner of a prospector turning over stones in search of gold. Later as a schoolboy I found that textbooks, though full of information, failed to provide answers to the burning questions I was asking. However, as an unsuspecting teenager, a book from a dusty attic opened the door that led me across the threshold into a goldmine of knowledge.

Along the way, I was joined in my work by Peter Hewitt, without whose insights, clarity and perseverance this book would never have been completed. A graduate in the history and philosophy of science, Peter introduced me to the fact that the vortex had once been at the forefront of scientific thinking about matter. At his own university, Cambridge, as well as in London, the vortex had been a torch upheld by an entire generation of British physicists, enabling them to look more deeply into the nature of reality than ever before.

Proposed by an extraordinary Scottish scientific genius in the 1860s, it had been endorsed by the most distinguished physicists of the late 19th century. However, by a tragic series of events at the beginning of the 20th century, this illumination was lost.

Peter and I wish to rekindle this torch. Neither of us is a professional scientist, nor do we enjoy the support and facilities of mainstream science.

But we believe that re-introducing the vortex today could lead to a profound re-evaluation of fundamentals. Our researches have convinced us that something vital is missing in physics and that the vortex is the key that has been overlooked. We believe that the vortex has the potential to transform physics and resolve many of the paradoxes that have grown up in this subject in the 20th century.

It seems to us that the vortex is the missing element in the present account of the physical universe. At the same time, it holds the key to understanding the non-physical. Science has traditionally denied the reality of anything non-material; the vortex opens the frontiers of science to the non-physical in a way never before possible. Bridging the gap between science and the supernatural, it sheds fresh light on mysteries that have puzzled mankind since time immemorial.

This book is a first presentation of these new ideas. Intended for people without any specialist knowledge, education or interest in science, it paints a broad picture, including only the minimum of essential physics. Within it a completely new science of the supernatural emerges.

David Ash, Dittisham, Devon 1990

Introduction

Is the supernatural real? Or is it, as many suppose, a mere residue of primitive belief? In times gone by, the reality of supernatural events and experiences was accepted as a matter of course. Yet today we call these phenomena paranormal, and treat them with doubt and disbelief. Challenging our understanding of the world, the supernatural is surrounded by scepticism.

The supernatural and paranormal are not rare and remote: these events and experiences are familiar to everyone. Dowsers locate water, minerals or missing persons. Healers perform seemingly miraculous cures. Astronauts and airline officers see UFOs. Clairvoyants predict future events. Hospital patients leave their bodies whilst under anaesthetic. Mothers know when a son or daughter is in danger, or dying, even when they are far away. Nearly everyone has received a phone call from a friend they have just been thinking about.

Many people would like to accept the paranormal and supernatural as real. But the dominant view of the world does not support them. Reports of supernatural and paranormal experiences are picked over and criticised. Every scrap of evidence is contested or argued way. Conditioned by materialism and traditional scientific views of the world, even religious believers find it hard to accept ideas of angels and life after death.

Science has found no place for the supernatural. It cannot accommodate the paranormal. In earlier centuries, scientific scepticism played a vital role in dispelling religious fear and superstition. But now the pendulum has swung too far; science has made it hard to believe in anything. We are drowning in a sea of doubt.

In this century, there have been many attempts to reconcile science with the supernatural. Some people have sought to find in contemporary physics a basis for man's traditional beliefs. But they have mainly taken for granted the scientific theories of their day.

Our approach is entirely different. Our starting point is a completely fresh picture of the natural world. This book is not another interpretation of the 'new physics'. Rather, we describe a wholly new view of the physical world, based on a crucial lost insight in physics. This single, simple key – discarded in the scientific turmoil at the start of the century – leads, we believe, to a new understanding of everything.

Probing more deeply into fundamentals, it offers the possibility of a new foundation for physics. At the same time, it opens the door to the supernatural. This new picture goes beyond the previous boundaries of science to embrace both the natural and the supernatural, the normal and the paranormal. Physics and metaphysics merge into a single science.

There are many books on the supernatural and paranormal which scrutinise the evidence and endeavour to prove the reality of these phenomena. We do not attempt to provide evidence for all the events and experiences we discuss. We do not expect everyone to believe in everything we cite; we have deliberately chosen examples of the supernatural and paranormal from contrasting traditions and beliefs. We are not seeking to support any particular religious creed; nor is it for us to tell people what to believe.

Our aim, rather, is to establish a framework in which the strange and miraculous become credible. The new picture points to a bridge between the physical and unseen, non-physical worlds. Many otherwise mysterious and inexplicable events become reasonable. Moreover, this new understanding of the supernatural reveals unsuspected dimensions to the natural, leading to a richer and more holistic appreciation of ourselves and our world.

Bringing together the findings of mystics and scientists, this picture enables us to relate in a new way to the totality of human experience. It shows that man is far more than a physical body and points to the unique opportunity offered by human life. Supporting many of man's traditional beliefs, it suggests that man is not an accident of evolution and that life after death and reincarnation are real possibilities. In it, gods and nature spirits, angels and demons, all have their place. As such, it is a science of the gods.

CHAPTER 1

Lord Kelvin's Vortex

It was a wintery day in Edinburgh, February 18th 1867. A distinguished Victorian gentleman was setting out for a very special evening. Although a bitter wind was blowing, the weather that late afternoon was fine, with no prospect of rain or snow. Pulling the collar of his coat about his ears, he decided to walk rather than take a cab.

He looked forward with pleasure to the lecture he was to give that evening. But his excitement was mixed with apprehension. What he had to say was completely new. It amounted to a revolution. How would his ideas be received? It was outrageous. He was on his way to speak to the Royal Society of Edinburgh – one of the most distinguished scientific audiences of his day – and he was going to cut the ground from right underneath their feet.

As he strode along, he was aware of the magnificent buildings that surrounded him. With their iron and granite, brass and stone, they epitomised everything that was solid and secure. His audience trusted in such things. They thought they knew where they stood with matter. He was going to tell them they were completely mistaken.

Like the frosty pavements beneath his feet, matter appeared to be something substantial. He aimed to show that it was nothing of the sort. Matter, in his view, had nothing concrete about it at all. It was no more substantial than the swirling Scottish mist that had, by now, completely engulfed him.

This man's vision has since been described as one of the most remarkable theories of its kind ever put forward. As the most original theory of matter in two and a half thousand years, it is hardly surprising that it caused a revolution. The ideas he launched that cold February night set into motion a ferment of activity that was to last to the end of the century.

Tragically, in the upheavals of the early 20th century, his ideas were lost. Revived today, his profound insight into the fundamental nature of matter could cause a new revolution, shattering our understanding of the material world and the physical universe.

Matter is our touchstone for what is real. But if the material world is not what we think it is, then everything changes. Everything is thrown into the air. With our ideas of reality exploded, everything we believe in comes into question.

The handsome Scotsman striding down the streets of Edinburgh was Sir William Thomson. Born in Belfast in 1824, he became one of the greatest physicists of his day. A child prodigy, Thomson entered Glasgow University at the age of eleven. He went on to Cambridge, where he became renowned for his original thinking. On returning to Glasgow, he was appointed professor at the age of only twenty-two.

During his life Thomson was heaped with honours. He pioneered the laying of the first successful trans-Atlantic cable. This achievement caught the public imagination and for it he was knighted in 1866. In 1890, he was elected President of the Royal Society, the most prestigious scientific body in the country. In 1892, he was elevated to the peerage, becoming Lord Kelvin. In 1902, in recognition of his outstanding achievements in science, he became a founder member of the Order of Merit. This honour, one of the most exclusive conferred by the British Crown, is restricted to the Sovereign and twenty-four men and women of great eminence. On his death in 1907, Lord Kelvin was buried in Westminster Abbey, next to Sir Isaac Newton.

Kelvin made major contributions in many leading areas of science and technology. He is perhaps most famous today as a founding father of thermodynamics. He was responsible for defining absolute zero and the Kelvin scale of temperature that is named after him. With the help of other scientists, he formulated the law of conservation of energy and did pioneering work on the kinetic theory of gases. He also worked extensively in the field of electricity and magnetism, inventing several ingenious instruments which are still in use – including the mirror galvanometer, the dynamometer, and the magnetically-shielded ship's compass.

Figure 1. William Thomson, the young professor, aged 22

It was a time of revolution. In Kelvin's day, the fabric of society was changing more rapidly than ever before. Railways were carving into the countryside. The industrial revolution was in full swing and whole populations were migrating from the country into the mushrooming towns with their mills, factories and endless terraces of houses. Everyone was on the move, everything was changing. Established ideas about the world and even life itself were being turned upside down.

It was Kelvin's destiny to challenge the established view of matter. His radical vision was in keeping with the revolutionary nature of his time.

In the 19th century it was generally accepted that matter consisted ultimately of atoms – solid, substantial particles. This idea of minute corpuscles of material had originated in the ancient world, in the teachings of the Greek philosophers Democritus and Epicurus, around 400 BC.

To understand the classical idea of the atom, imagine a lump of wood. A small piece is cut out of it. Then this piece itself is divided into smaller and smaller bits. The idea was that one would end up, ultimately, with a tiny piece of material that could not be divided any further. This final and most fundamental *atom* of matter was thought to be completely indestructible.

None of the writings of Democritus and Epicurus have survived. However their ideas were passed on by the Roman poet Lucretius (99-55 BC). Lost in the Dark Ages but rediscovered in the Renaissance, his work inspired the natural philosophers of the 17th and 18th centuries who laid the foundations of modern science. The most celebrated of them, Sir Isaac Newton, lent his authority to the corpuscular concept when he wrote, "It seems to me probable that God in the beginning formed matter in solid, hard, impenetrable, movable particles."

This picture of the underlying nature of matter had a profound influence. It provided a view of a mechanical universe, composed solely of little particles in perpetual motion. The atoms themselves were thought of as tiny solid spheres, like minute billiard balls.

In the 19th century, the vast majority of scientists embraced this idea, which formed the bedrock of scientific materialism.

Kelvin was a dissident. He was prepared to take on the entire scientific establishment of his day. His new vision of matter challenged the concept of the 'billiard ball' atom. Kelvin believed in basic atomic theory. He accepted that everything was made up of atoms. However, he found it ridiculous to assume that atoms were solid material particles.

His reasoning was simple. At that time, atoms were thought to be substantial particles with certain fixed properties. Their properties were then used to explain the characteristics of matter as a whole.

For example, atoms were taken to be perfectly elastic, so that they could bounce off each other. Elastic collisions between atoms were vital to explain the behaviour of gases. However, nobody explained *why* atoms were elastic in the first place. Scientists simply assumed that elasticity was an *inherent* property of atoms. They took it for granted that that was the end of the story.

Kelvin found this attitude superficial and naive. He wanted to go further. Unlike his predecessors and contemporaries, he wasn't prepared to take the properties of atoms for granted. Kelvin wanted to explain the properties of atoms in terms of something more fundamental.

The reality was that scientists could not account for anything about the atom. They could not say why atoms were permanent and stable. Nor did they understand how their other characteristics – such as elasticity – arose. They simply assumed that all these properties were basic attributes of the atom.

To Kelvin this was a "monstrous assumption". He believed that the properties of atoms could be *reduced* to something more fundamental.

In 1867, Kelvin found the key. Having puzzled for many years, he was rewarded, according to his biographer, with "a flash of inspiration". He saw that there was a simple explanation in terms of a single underlying principle.

Kelvin was sure that he had the answer. Moreover he had a simple way of demonstrating it. Today, physicists demand billions of dollars for equipment to demonstrate their ideas about the fundamental nature of matter. Kelvin's apparatus consisted of a couple of boxes, two towels and a few flasks of chemicals.

One side of each box was closed by a stout towel stretched tightly across it. In the opposite side was a circular hole. Within each box, thick clouds of smoke were produced by mixing the vapours of an acid with ammonia. When a firm blow was struck on the towel, a circular smoke ring shot out from the hole on the opposite side. Smoke rings could be blown out simultaneously from the two boxes.

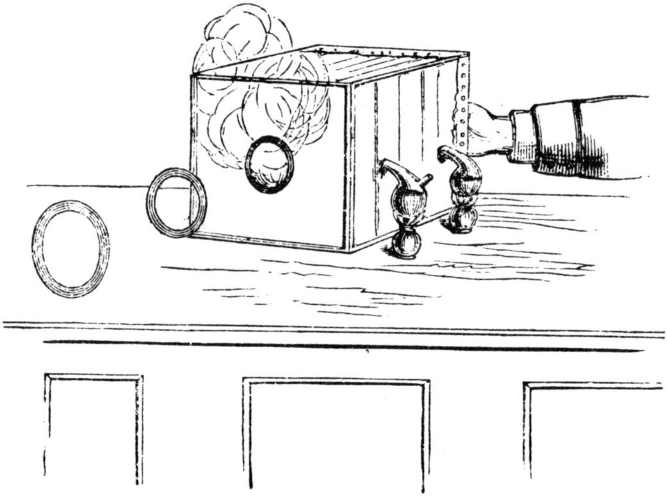

Figure 2. Vortex rings produced by a smoke box

These rings behaved quite remarkably. On hitting each other, they didn't merge or break up, as one might expect. Instead, as they sped across the room and collided, they bounced off each other, shaking violently from the shock of the impact. It was as if they were two rubber rings, striking one another in the air. Insubstantial whirls of smoke were behaving as if they were substantial objects. They couldn't even be cut with a knife; they simply moved away from the blade, or wriggled around it.

This demonstration was central to Kelvin's startling new vision of matter. It showed that two smoke rings acted on each other much like elastic objects. These smoke rings had many of the properties attributed to atoms. They exhibited resilience and inertia. They were surprisingly stable and durable. At the same time, they were elastic.

Kelvin pointed out that these *vortex rings* of smoke behaved just like atoms. They gave the appearance of being quite substantial. But this apparent solidity was an illusion which came from vortex spin.

Kelvin concluded that atoms were nothing more nor less than vortex rings. Thus he gave birth to the *vortex atom.*

In Kelvin's view, all the properties of atoms stemmed from vortex spin. Their substantiality was a masquerade. It was movement in a vortex that gave rise to the illusion of material.

Kelvin's vision of the atom as a vortex was brilliant. In a single stroke, it rendered obsolete the whole tradition of the atom as the ultimate little bit of material. The ultimate particles of matter, far from being solid and substantial, were merely vortices.

Kelvin's vortex theory became outstandingly successful. But he did have problems to overcome.

The first concerned the permanence of matter. Vortices are common throughout the natural world. Tornadoes, hurricanes and whirlpools are examples. Fast-spinning vortices are remarkably persistent forms; even slow-moving smoke rings have surprising durability. But in nature, vortices don't last forever. They dissipate and eventually die away.

Matter, however, is stable; it doesn't just fall apart and dissolve away. Atoms are forever. If vortices were to be the basis of matter, they would have to be permanent. The motion forming them would have to continue unchanged, indefinitely. How was this perpetual motion possible?

Then there was another question. Vortices normally occur in fluids. Hurricanes are in the air and tidal whirlpools are in water. What was the atom a vortex *in*?

There was a single, obvious answer to both these questions. The vital clue came from a German physicist called Herman von Helmholtz (1821-1894). A few years earlier Helmholtz was studying vortices in liquids when he came up with an amazing discovery. It was very simple: if the liquid was frictionless, the vortices would not disintegrate or die away; they would last forever.

Kelvin was a friend of Helmholtz; they had worked together in the past. When Kelvin learnt of Helmholtz' discovery, he was immensely excited. He realised at once that the permanence of the atom could stem from endless vortex motion in a frictionless fluid.

It had long been believed in physics that the universe was filled with exactly such a frictionless fluid – the aether. The aether was thought of as a subtle, invisible substance pervading everything, even empty space.

In Kelvin's day, the existence of the aether was vital to explain light. Light was regarded as waves and a wave, it was argued, had to be a wave *in something*. Waves in the sea are movements of water. If light was a wave, there must be some underlying substance moving. This hypothetical substance, filling the whole of space and even permeating solid matter, was the aether.

Kelvin realised that he could put forward a unified theory of matter and light, explaining them both in terms of the aether. He could account for the entire physical universe simply in terms of waves and vortices. Light was a wave motion in the aether, while matter was a vortex motion.

The vortex atom came in with a bang. From his historic lecture in 1867 came Kelvin's first paper on vortex atoms. Later that year, again at the Royal Society of Edinburgh, he presented a mathematical dissertation on vortex motion. Kelvin went on to advocate the vortex atom for most of his professional life.

The vortex quickly attracted the support of major British scientists. Many became convinced that it was the key to understanding matter. Within a very few years, the idea of the vortex became firmly established. A whole school of British physics grew up around the vortex atom, centred in the universities of London and Cambridge. Many notable physicists worked in this field, building up a mathematical picture of the vortex atom and its interactions.

The year 1875 was a landmark in popular acceptance of the vortex. The new edition of the *Encyclopaedia Britannica* devoted two entire pages to Kelvin's vortex. Its entry on *The Atom* reviewed the whole history of atomic ideas, including the previous picture of a *"small, hard body imagined by Lucretius, and endorsed by Newton"*. The article concluded that the vortex theory was far superior to any of its predecessors, stating:

> . . . the vortex ring of Helmholtz, imagined as the true form of the atom by Thomson, satisfies more of the conditions than any atom hitherto imagined.

The author of this article was none other than James Clerk Maxwell (1831-1879), himself a giant of 19th century physics. Maxwell was another Scottish child prodigy. One of his papers was published by the Royal Society when he was only fifteen. Ten years later, at twenty-five, he was appointed professor at the University of Aberdeen. He went on to become the first ever professor of experimental physics at Cambridge, where he established the now famous Cavendish laboratory.

Maxwell was one of the greatest geniuses of the 19th century. He is most celebrated for his development of electromagnetic theory – without which there would be no television, radio or radar. Probably the leading mathematical physicist of the 19th

Figure 3. James Clerk Maxwell as a young man

century, his grasp of this subject was so fundamental that his equations have survived intact to this day.

Maxwell was a major advocate of the vortex. He was convinced that it was by far the best explanation for matter that had ever been put forward.

Another celebrated scientist who championed the vortex atom was Sir J J Thomson (1856-1940). Twenty-five years younger, J J Thomson followed in Maxwell's footsteps as professor of experimental physics at Cambridge. Through his work, he made the Cavendish the greatest experimental physics laboratory in the world. Like his namesake Lord Kelvin, J J Thomson was extensively honoured. He was President of the Royal Society, was knighted for his contributions to science, and was admitted to the Order of Merit. Eventually, like Kelvin, he was buried in Westminster Abbey.

Sir J J Thomson is famous for his discovery of the electron, the basis of electricity, electronics and computers. In 1882,

Figure 4. Sir J J Thomson in the Cavendish Laboratory

whilst still a promising young man at Cambridge, he won the Adams prize with a paper on the motion of vortex rings. This essay gave a detailed mathematical treatment of the vortex. It also indicated how chemical reactions could be explained in terms of the vortex atom. In his paper, J J Thomson said of the vortex atom that it

> . . . has *a priori* very strong recommendations in its favour . . . the vortex theory of matter is of a much more fundamental character than the ordinary solid particle theory.

J J Thomson published several further papers on the vortex and continued to endorse vortex theories for over a quarter of a century.

Kelvin's original picture of the vortex atom evolved considerably over the years. During the last decades of the century, different groups of physicists developed several alternative models in considerable mathematical detail. They looked to the vortex to provide a single model capable of explaining everything that was then known in physics and chemistry.

With the 20th century everything changed. This vibrant school of British physics came to a sudden end. Explosions in the fabric of science rocked it to its very foundations. The atom was split and the idea of the aether was dying. The atom came under new, intense scrutiny, and all existing ideas about it proved to be completely inadequate.

The vortex idea, with all its enormous potential, was thrown away along with the moribund billiard ball model. But the baby was chucked out with the bath water. It is time to look again at the vortex. Today, in the light of everything that has been discovered, this forgotten principle could provide a completely new foundation for science.

CHAPTER 2

The Vortex of Energy

On a summer morning in 1945 an atomic bomb exploded over Hiroshima. This was a terrible demonstration for mankind of the enormous power locked up in the atom. In this atomic explosion, less than an ounce of matter had been transformed into sufficient energy to destroy the entire city.

Albert Einstein, forty years earlier, was responsible for the breakthrough which made the atom bomb possible. By showing that matter was equivalent to energy, he paved the way for both the atomic bomb and nuclear power.

This is the most crucial scientific discovery of the century. But the equivalence of matter and energy is baffling. It is the greatest enigma of 20th century physics. Modern physics is still grappling to understand precisely what matter is and why it appears to be interchangeable with energy. How can matter, seemingly so static, be a form of energy, which is intrinsically dynamic?

Only a few years after Einstein's discovery, the atom itself came under attack. Physicists killed off the traditional idea of the atom as the smallest indivisible piece of matter. The billiard ball atom was shattered. The atom was found to be made up of much smaller, sub-atomic particles.

Today, the atom, so far from being seen as a solid indestructible mass, is known to be largely empty space. It consists of Sir J J Thomson's tiny electrons orbiting a central nucleus made up of further particles. It would be tempting to imagine that these *elementary particles* are themselves solid billiard ball-like objects. But modern physics has shown quite clearly that they are destructible and can be totally transformed into energy.

The traditional notion that matter is made up of indestructible material particles is obviously false. But the question then is, just what are elementary particles? And how can they be forms

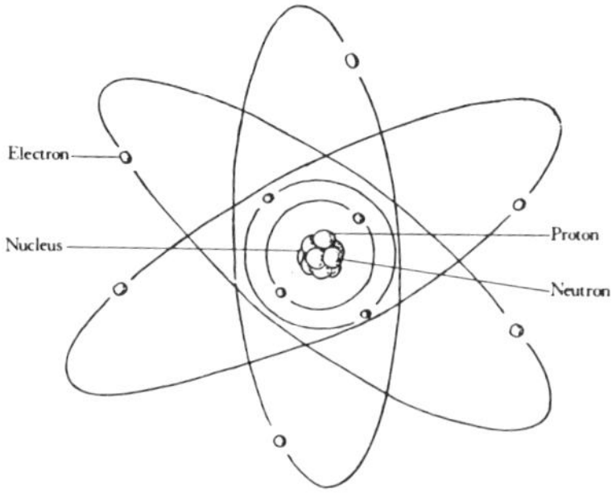

Figure 5. The traditional picture of the atom with its constitute elementary particles

of energy? For most of this century, physics has been puzzling over these problems.

Kelvin's vortex provides the answer. The vortex is the key to understanding the precise structure of particles, and how energy is locked up in them.

To Lord Kelvin and his contemporaries, the atom was the elementary particle – the smallest particle of matter. It was natural, therefore, that he applied his vortex model to the atom.

Today, however, sub-atomic particles are taken to be the smallest bits of matter. If Kelvin were alive now, he would seek to explain particles, not atoms. He would be publishing papers on vortex particles, not on vortex atoms!

In 1884, Kelvin gave a famous series of lectures in America on the wave theory of light. In his day, it was thought that light consisted of waves in the aether – the invisible substance supposed to pervade all space. Kelvin, like his contemporaries, believed in the aether. It is logical therefore that he took atoms to be vortices in the aether.

Later, however, physicists came to view light very differently.

The underlying sea of aether was completely dismissed. Physicists came to accept that waves of energy could exist with no underlying material to move. Waves could exist without the ocean – like the grin on the face of the Cheshire cat which stayed behind even after the cat had vanished.

A vortex theory today has no need of the aether; indeed any mention of the aether would be scientific suicide. A claim that particles were vortices in the aether would be taken as ludicrous. But if you can have a wave of pure energy, why not a vortex?

Kelvin was so close. He was after all a founding father of thermodynamics, the science of energy. If only he had talked about energy, not aether! His theory would then make perfect sense today. Its foundation would be:

an elementary particle is a vortex of energy.

This is a simple idea. But it has immense power. If the elementary particle is a vortex of energy, our understanding of the world would be completely transformed.

For a start, the vortex resolves the most fundamental enigma of modern physics. It shows for the first time how energy is locked up in matter. Einstein described matter as *frozen energy*. The vortex gives a much clearer picture: movement is the very foundation of matter – there is nothing 'frozen' in it at all.

Now we can really see what Einstein meant when he said that mass is equivalent to energy.

It is ironic that at the turn of the century, just as Einstein was predicting the equivalence of mass and energy, the idea of the vortex went out of vogue. The achievement of the vortex is to portray matter as energy. It makes Einstein's idea intelligible, by describing the form that energy takes in matter.

Energy is not material. There is no sea of energy like the aether. It is not some *stuff* or some fluid that flows. Energy is dynamic, it is action and change. We could picture energy as movement.

Just as movement cannot exist without direction, so energy cannot exist without form. It is not that energy *forms* the vortex or the wave. The vortex *is* energy. The two fundamental forms of energy in our world are matter and light. Light is often taken to be a wave form of energy. We are suggesting that matter is a vortex. Just as waves of light can exist without an aether to wave in, so matter is not a vortex *in* anything; it is pure energy, with no material moving.

In nature, most vortices are conical in shape. Tornadoes and whirlpools are swirling cones. These natural phenomena well illustrate the dynamic nature of the vortex particle. But they completely fail to show its form. Elementary particles are best thought of as spheres, not cones.

Neither do Kelvin's smoke rings give us an accurate picture of the vortex of energy. Smoke rings have sides. The vortex of energy, to form an elementary particle, must be spherical and symmetric.

For an elementary particle, we need a *spherical vortex*, one that is completely symmetric. The vortex particle cannot be a cone or a ring; it must be a ball – a ball of energy. But how could a ball of energy arise? How could a spherical vortex be formed out of movement? Picture movement as a line. If a line is wound freely in a spiral, it creates a ball. Likewise, movement in a spiral could form a spherical vortex – a ball of swirling energy.

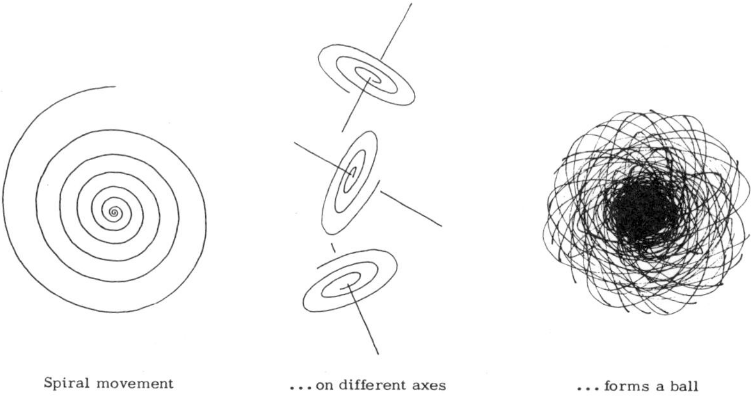

Figure 6. The vortex: spiral movement in three dimensions forms a swirling ball of energy

The vortex of energy could be pictured as a ball of wool. In a ball of wool, wool winds in a three-dimensional spiral around a single point. In the spherical vortex, there would be a similar spiral spin around a central point. A ball of wool is normally static. Only when being wound up or unwound would it accurately portray the vortex of energy.

It is easy to see from this that there could be two totally opposite types of vortex forming sub-atomic particles. One would be winding up; the other would be unwinding. With continuous movement in the vortex, like water in a whirlpool, the particle would stay the same size.

The vortex of energy is a simple image of great power. The vortex shows how something as dynamic as energy can underlie something as static as matter. Spin creates stability. Just as Kelvin's lively smoke rings appeared to be resilient objects, so vortices of energy could masquerade as stable and substantial particles.

This model helps us to understand how matter can be transformed into energy. What happens when you unravel a ball of wool? You fill the room with wool. If you could unravel a vortex of energy, an enormous quantity of energy would be released. Just as a ball of wool is a very compact form of wool, so a vortex particle is a very concentrated form of energy.

Many properties of matter can be explained very simply using the vortex.

One puzzling aspect of matter is the mysterious forces which appear to arise from it. Everyone is familiar with these forces. Take magnetism for instance. We all know how iron filings cling to a magnet. Electric charge is another fundamental force in nature. Little bits of paper will cling onto a charged piece of plastic such as a comb.

These forces are very real and very powerful. But they have never been easy for science to explain. If particles of matter are inert blobs of material, how can they act on each other?

The vortex offers an elegant explanation for these forces. Vortices of energy are intrinsically dynamic. Should they overlap, it is obvious that they would interact with each other. In this way, the vortex gets *underneath* matter and begins to show *why* it has the properties it displays.

The vortex does not challenge the findings of classical and modern physics. Rather it establishes a new foundation for them. It helps us to understand the inner nature of matter and the mysterious forces associated with it. In physics and chemistry, science has explored the laws which govern the interactions of atoms and molecules. The idea that an elementary particle is a vortex of energy does not alter these macroscopic facts. Instead, the new vortex model could serve to underpin and unify the natural laws that have been discovered, by pointing to the underlying reality from which they arise.

The great majority of people have been completely put off physics because it is so difficult to comprehend. However, with the fresh understanding provided by the vortex the complexity of this subject melts away. The vortex makes physics clear and accessible, bringing a comprehension of the physical world within the scope of everyone.

Despite its innate simplicity, the vortex can begin to resolve the mysteries of physics. Understanding sub-atomic particles as vortices of energy begins to remove the paradoxes associated with them. It makes their properties and behaviour much easier to understand. Features of the physical universe that science has taken as impenetrable can now be explained.

Electric charge, for example, was previously taken to be an *irreducible* property of matter. Likewise, the existence of just two types of electric charge has been taken for granted and treated as inexplicable. But these features of matter can also be explained by the vortex. As we have already seen, the spherical vortex can form in two completely opposite ways: in one, the spin is into the centre; in the other, it is out. These two forms correspond to *positive* and *negative* electric charges.

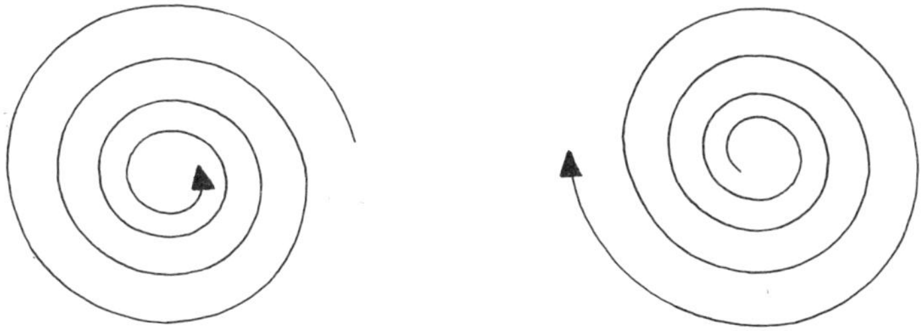

Figure 7. The two types of electric charge – positive and negative, arise from the two types of vortex – winding up and unwinding

Furthermore, the vortex makes it clear why there are just two types of electric charge in the universe and not one, or four.

There are many more puzzles in physics that the vortex can solve. Even such basic concepts as mass can be explained: mass is a measure of the quantity of energy in spin. As we shall later, the vortex also gives an account of the nature of space and time.

The vortex could achieve in 20th century physics what Lord Kelvin sought to achieve in the 19th century. Kelvin wanted to delve more deeply into the mysteries of matter than his contemporaries. He wanted to know what lay underneath matter and behind it – what really made it tick. He set out to look beneath the surface. In the vortex, he found a unifying and explanatory principle of immense power. Kelvin's vortex atom was moving toward a unification of 19th century physics. In the 20th century, the vortex particle could serve the same purpose. It could provide the basis of the all-embracing theory that modern physics has been searching for.

Athough it is beyond the scope of this book to develop this theme. The two major pillars of 20th century physics are Relativity and Quantum theory. As the concept of the vortex is developed, it appears to complement major areas of both these achievements.

In Quantum theory, for example, it can begin to provide models which give physical reality to otherwise obscure concepts. Take, for instance, the enigma of quantum spin. Quantum theory regards this elusive property as somehow intrinsic to the particle, but insists that it is not a form of particle rotation. The vortex shows quite clearly that spin is absolutely intrinsic to the particle, being fundamental to its very existence.

With regard to Relativity, the vortex account for space, outlined in a later chapter, is entirely compatible with Einstein's theory and goes on to illuminate it in a quite unexpected way.

The vortex is the final nail in the coffin of materialism.

What is matter? And why does it behave the way it does? Traditionally, in natural philosophy, the properties of matter were taken to derive from an underlying *material substance* that was durable, inactive and resistant to change.

Kelvin struck the first blow. He was able to explain many aspects of matter through the vortex. It was no longer necessary to suppose that the properties of matter came from some underlying material *stuff*. They arose from vortex movement. But Kelvin's vortex still required the aether – itself a material substance.

The vortex of energy dispenses with material entirely. It complements Einstein by showing that matter is pure energy masquerading as material. The vortex explains away all the supposed properties of material. The requirement for any kind of substance to underpin the physical universe disappears completely.

Matter presents itself to us as the epitome of what is real. We use the phrase 'as solid as a rock'. Yet our senses mislead us. Rocks, though real, are far from solid. Matter is mainly empty space with a few particles buzzing around in it. If these particles themselves are nothing but vortex movement, then it would seem that there isn't much in matter apart from pure movement.

The vortex unites the views of mystics and scientists. Mystics have always recognised that the world has no substance. Centuries before Kelvin, the Buddha described forms of matter as whirlpools in a busy stream. Yogi philosophers realised that '*matter is but a vortex of energy*'. For thousands of years, it has been taught in the East that the world is an illusion – the illusion of *maya*. The vortex shows clearly how the illusion is created.

CHAPTER 3

Key to the Supernatural

A guest at a party tells you that he can recall a past life. Do you take him seriously, or do you just smile?

A girl claims to have seen a ghost or a fairy. How do you react? Do you accept the possibility that she may have seen something real? Or do you assume that she must be simple-minded or over-impressionable?

Your aunt tells you that she has been miraculously cured by a healer. Can you believe her? Or do you suspect it must all have been in her mind in the first place?

If a friend told you that, during an operation, he found himself floating up to the ceiling, looking down on the surgeons operating on his body, would you believe him? Or would you think he must have been hallucinating?

If someone told you that they had seen a UFO, what would you think? Would you accept what they said? Or would you assume they were too ignorant to recognise a weather balloon?

Many people find it difficult to accept the supernatural and paranormal. Events are treated with suspicion and scepticism. Accounts are picked over and criticised. Every scrap of evidence is contested. Some people explain away past-life memories as extra-sensory perception. Others dismiss ESP itself as mere coincidence. Apparitions are taken to be mere fantasies and miraculous cures as being all in the mind. Everything magical is reduced to the mundane.

Just what is the supernatural? Does it all come from overheated imagination? Is it all superstition and wishful thinking? Or is it for real?

The vortex holds the key. The vortex leads to a coherent account of the supernatural, paranormal and psychic. Many otherwise strange and mysterious experiences can be quickly and simply explained. The vortex provides a framework which enables us to accept the supernatural as reality.

Realising that our world is nothing but energy is the crucial step. Energy is the prime reality. Energy is the foundation of everything in the universe, from the minute atom to the mighty galaxy.

But is the physical universe the only reality? If matter and light – its building blocks – are purely two forms of energy, could there be other energy, in non-material forms?

It was Einstein who first established the relationship between matter and energy. His famous equation $E=mc^2$, shows that mass (m) is equivalent to energy (E). The vortex goes further: it shows the precise form of energy in matter. A particle of matter is a swirling ball of energy, a spherical vortex of movement.

Light is a different form of energy, but it is obvious from Einstein's equation that matter and light share a common movement. In $E=mc^2$, it is c, the speed of light, which relates matter to energy.

From this, we can draw a simple conclusion. It is obvious: the speed of movement in matter must be the speed of light. This is the only possible sense we can make of Einstein's equation.

If, in a particle of matter, the vortex movement is at the speed of light, we could picture the particle as a minute fireball, a spiral at the speed of light.

But would the vortex always be restricted to the speed of light? Could the movement in it ever be faster? We have equated energy with movement. Is all movement constrained by the speed of light?

Science has come to the conclusion that nothing can move faster than the speed of light. This rule applies to all forms of energy – including particles of matter and light. But does it apply to the movement that underlies energy itself, the primal movement from which matter and light themselves arise?

This is the crucial question. It all boils down to what energy is. Whilst physicists will not commit themselves to saying what energy is, they are adamant that energy cannot move faster than the speed of light. But if forms of energy are intrinsically forms of movement, then movement is more fundamental than energy.

Figure 8. Albert Einstein

Why should pure movement be limited to the speed of light?

If movement could have a faster speed, it would give rise to a completely different type of energy. This we could call *super-energy.*

Energy and super-energy would be different in substance. Movement at the speed of light could be described as the *substance* of energy in the physical world. The substance of super-energy would be movement at a faster speed.

Super-energy might well behave like energy. For example there could be vortices of super-energy, akin to particles of matter, and waves of super-energy, akin to light. Together they could establish a *super-physical* reality.

Objects of super-energy could share the same *form* as things in our world, but their *substance* would be entirely different. Matter would not interact with them. Light would not reflect off them. Presenting no obstruction to matter or light whatsoever, they would be completely intangible and invisible.

Such objects would not be available to any of the five normal human senses. Their presence would be difficult or even impossible to detect. Scientific evidence for their existence would be hard to establish. Many people might refuse to accept that such super-physical forms existed, because they could not experience them with their senses. However, forms of energy beyond light might exist all around us, and move unobstructed right through us, without most of us even being aware of them.

These concepts start to make some sense of the paranormal. Take ghosts, for example. Ghosts are often said to be of a different 'substance' to matter. They are supposed to pass with ease through solid walls. They also seem to exist outside our time. Could they be forms of super-energy, existing just beyond our space and time?

Super-energy would not occupy our space and time. Super-physical forms could not be part of our normal reality. They would be quite distinct and separate. This is clear from Relativity.

To Einstein, the speed of light was the most fundamental thing in the physical universe. In Relativity, he treated it as "the sole universal constant" and showed that everything in our world – including space and time – is related to this speed. Approaching the speed of light, extraordinary things begin to happen to space and time. Space is foreshortened and time intervals grow longer. At the speed of light itself, time disappears into eternity and space collapses on itself.

It must be clear from this that movements faster than the speed of light are impossible in the space-time of our world. For this reason, super-energy could not be part of the physical universe; super-physical forms – 'bodies' of super-energy – would transcend our space and time.

Super-energy in the vortex could account for many reported paranormal phenomena. One important class of event it might explain is strange vanishings and materialisations. Many things far more substantial than ghosts have been known to appear or disappear quite inexplicably. Religion and legend are littered with stories in which people and objects mysteriously vanish – or 'pop up' unexpectedly. Reports of similar events continue even in our present time. These phenomena cannot be explained away as illusions or the tricks of stage magicians. They have no explanation in science. However with the concepts of the vortex and super-energy, we can begin to offer an account of them.

Every object in our world consists of billions of elementary particles arranged into atoms and molecules. We have pictured each particle as a vortex of energy in which the underlying movement is at the speed of light.

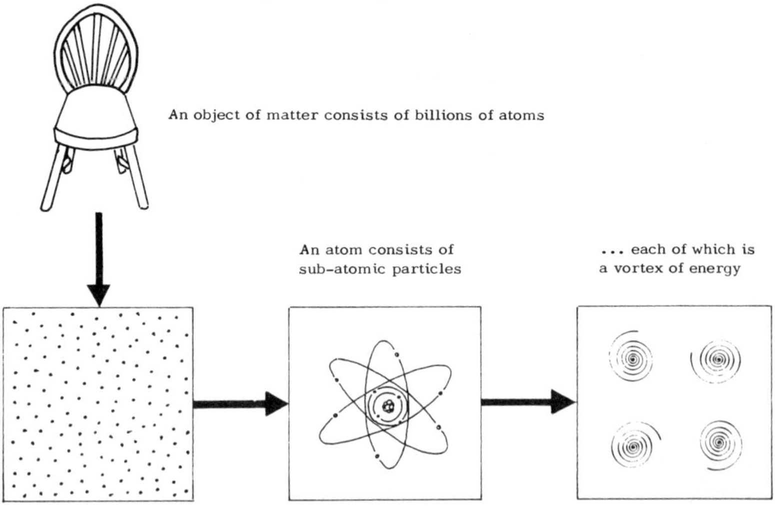

Figure 9. Everyday objects consist of billions of vortices of energy

Suppose this movement in the vortex should speed up. Exceeding the speed of light, the energy would immediately become super-energy. Changing in substance, the object would suddenly cease to interact with matter and light. Instantly it would become both invisible and intangible. It would not 'move off' anywhere, but it would cease to be perceived.

This procedure could be reversed. Movement in the vortices could be slowed down again to the speed of light. Super-energy would revert to energy. The object would immediately reappear.

This process could appropriately be described as *transubstantiation*, reflecting the change in substance of energy to super-energy.

Transubstantiation is vital to understanding the paranormal. It is the bridge between the natural and the supernatural, between the physical and the super-physical. Science is concerned mainly with the changing *forms* of energy. We are concerned more with the *substance* of energy. It becomes possible to dismantle the barrier between the natural and the supernatural, the normal and the paranormal.

Through transubstantiation, an object could *materialise* or *dematerialise*. Dematerialisation is not dissolution. A dematerialised object would be invisible and intangible. But it would be no less real than it was. The object would simply have changed in substance to become super-physical.

The speed of light is the limit of the physical universe. It could be described as the 'boundary' of our world. Transubstantiation would take an object through this *light-barrier* and into the realm of the super-physical. The light-barrier would be the dividing line between the physical and the super-physical. It would demarcate the natural from the supernatural.

In the early days of jets, the speed of sound was thought to be the maximum speed anyone could attain. Pilots believed their aircraft would break up if they went any faster. Eventually, however, test pilots broke through the *sound-barrier*, and found themselves coming out alive on the other side.

Breaking through the light-barrier may appear daunting. However, there is no reason why it should be in any way destructive. Transubstantiation only affects the substance of an object, not its form. It would not change the atomic or molecular structure of a body. Even a living organism could break through the light-barrier without damage or disruption to its tissues and life processes.

Those who read J R Tolkien will find an echo of these ideas in his books *The Hobbit* and *Lord of the Rings*. In them, Tolkien conceived of a ring which made its wearer disappear from view. One could imagine that the ring had the power to take the wearer through the light-barrier. When the hobbit put the ring on his finger, he became invisible to his enemies. The misty world that he entered could be taken as the super-physical realm beyond the light-barrier. Without 'moving off' anywhere, he would appear to vanish as light passed right through the now empty space where his body was. The form of his body would be completely unaltered by transubstantiation; only the speed of movement within its vortices would be changed. Their form – in atoms and molecules, blood, skin and bone – would remain precisely the same.

The hobbit is fiction. But in history there are many purportedly factual accounts of people mysteriously vanishing, sometimes to reappear in completely different places. Take, for example, Apollonius of Tyana, a Greek philosopher said to have been an adept of the Pythagorean mystery schools. Accredited with extraordinary powers, his life and reported miracles have been compared with those of Christ, with whom he was contemporary. Accused in Rome of high treason, Apollonius was arrested and had to stand trial before Caesar. He was faced with almost certain execution. However, in the middle of his trial – to the amazement of the Emperor and everyone else – he suddenly and mysteriously vanished. He reappeared the same day in Puteoli, normally three days journey from Rome, and went on to live to the ripe old age of 101.

Christ himself, of course, is reported to have disappeared in a similar way on many occasions. The Gospels contain numerous examples; faced with threatening or overwhelming crowds, Christ would vanish from the 'midst of the multitude' and slip away unnoticed. It is easy to gloss over the enormity of such an event, but it would be equivalent in our day to a major public figure – perhaps the Pope or Michael Jackson – vanishing from view in front of a large gathering of people. Christ is several times reported to have appeared out of nowhere, which would have had a similar impact.

Tradition also has it that Christ rose from the dead – vanishing out of the tomb, and subsequently appearing to his disciples behind closed doors. Was Christ a master of transubstantiation, able to change the substance of his body at will? If so, he would have been able to materialise and dematerialise whenever he choose – perhaps even after clinical death. Christ eventually vanished with his body out of our world altogether, in the event described as his ascension into heaven. We could understand this to mean that, passing through the light-barrier for the last time, he entered a permanent super-physical existence. This would also suggest that heaven is the Biblical name for realms of super-energy existing beyond the speed of light.

In the Muslim tradition, Mohammed is credited with similar powers. He is said on one occasion to have mysteriously vanished from Mecca, and turned up on Mount Moriah in Jerusalem. This spot, regarded as sacred, is now covered by the Dome of the Rock. He subsequently disappeared from Jerusalem and reappeared in Mecca. On his return, Mohammed announced that he had passed through heaven on this remarkable journey transcending space and time.

Even in our own time, there are intriguing reports of saints mysteriously coming and going. In India, a Yogi known as Babaji is said to have materialised in the late 1960s to pass on an ancient breathing technique – now the basis of the practice called *rebirthing*. Then he vanished, leaving no trace. Followers believe that he has appeared on Earth with the same body many times over the centuries; he has been identified as the teacher of Yogananda's guru, Sri Yukteswar, in the 19th century.

CHAPTER 4
Modern Miracle Man

There is a vast body of evidence worldwide relating to paranormal phenomena. But the difficulties inherent in investigating this subject have never been fully overcome. Events are usually sporadic and unpredictable. Mostly they occur spontaneously, in circumstances that are difficult or impossible to reproduce. Many experiences are psychic in nature and not easily confirmed in repeatable scientific experiments. All of this makes the paranormal notoriously difficult to prove.

In this century, there have been several attempts to probe into the paranormal scientifically. Hauntings and the subtle energies associated with stone circles have been investigated with instruments. Researchers have brought psychics into the laboratory in an effort to show that their parapsychological powers are real. But the opportunity to investigate paranormal phenomena under controlled experimental conditions is rare.

Moreover the range of phenomena that can be studied in this way is limited.

Many researchers now accept that, rather than try to bring phenomena into the laboratory, they must go out into the field to investigate them as and when they occur.

It is in this spirit that two well-known researchers into the paranormal have made visits to India to investigate the purported abilities of a famous Indian holy man, Sri Sathya Sai Baba. Now in his early sixties, Sai Baba is a spiritual teacher with a large following around the world. He was born and still lives in a tiny village in Southern India.

Sai Baba has shown what appear to be extraordinary powers since the age of about 14. The range of his purported feats is very large, resembling those attributed to Christ in the New Testament. His followers describe cases of apparently miraculous healing, accurate prophesy and clairvoyance. He seems to

Figure 10. Sri Sathya Sai Baba

be able to read people's minds, giving complete strangers details of their past, present and future life. He is also said to appear in different places at the same time. But he is undoubtedly most celebrated for materialisations – his ability to make objects appear and disappear at will.

Many reports of mysterious appearances and disappearances are difficult to substantiate, or can be readily explained away. However the Sai Baba phenomena are not so easily dismissed. They are witnessed regularly by a great many people, in conditions which make trickery difficult or impossible. Sceptical scientists, hoping to find common-sense explanations, have testified to their conviction that Sai Baba's reported powers are genuine.

Dr Erlandur Haraldsson and Dr Karlis Osis made the first of several visits to study Sai Baba in 1973. Haraldsson, Professor of Psychology at the University of Iceland, has long been active in the field of psychic research and is the author of numerous books and articles. Osis is Chester F. Carlson Research Fellow of the American Society for Psychic Research in New York.

Haraldsson and Osis focused their attention on materialisation, being the most prominent and distinctive of the phenomena associated with Sai Baba. At the same time, these manifestations are the most challenging to science. Some so-called miracles are explained away as hallucinations. But when tangible objects, often of solid gold and precious stones, regularly appear out of nowhere, and are still in people's possession years later, it is hard to dismiss the whole thing as delusion.

Haraldsson and Osis published a joint report on their observations in the Journal of the American Society for Psychic Research in 1977. Their report is quoted here at some length because it gives an excellent description of typical Sai Baba materialisations, along with a considered opinion on them.

The report begins with an introduction to materialisation phenomena in general.

> Ostensibly paranormal appearances and disappearances of objects have been reported in various cultures. The phenomenon consists of objects appearing or disappearing in circumstances where no physical cause of the event can be detected. In cases where paranormal creation of the object is assumed, the process is usually referred to as a materiali-

sation. When an already existing object is 'brought' by paranormal means from one place to another without visible means of travel, the phenomenon is called teleportation and the object is referred to as an apport. Teleportation is said to occur in poltergeist cases. Materialisations of human forms have been reported in the presence of mediums . . .

The appearance and disappearance of objects is, of course, one of the favourite illusions created by stage magicians. With the help of astonishing dexterity, diversion of attention and some gadgetry, objects have 'appeared' and 'disappeared' on the magic show stage without detection of the tricks of the trade by the audience. Enterprising showmen throughout history have produced 'spirits' and 'demons' in religious settings in their claim to demonstrate 'supernatural' phenomena.

On close scrutiny, the bulk of the claims for materialisation and teleportation have been explained in quite natural (and sometimes entertaining) ways. Nevertheless, there are a few reports which keep the question open. On the whole, however, and in spite of considerable research done in this area by psychic researchers early in this century, claims of materialisation and allied phenomena have generally been frowned upon and rejected by nearly all present-day parapsychologists.

We, too, shared this point of view and did not give serious consideration to such phenomena until our encounters with Sri Sathya Sai Baba.

In the course of several meetings with Sai Baba, Haraldsson and Osis witnessed over twenty instances of materialisation – often observing at close range as the objects appeared.

The first thing the scientists saw appear was *vibuti*, a fine ash-like powder. At the time they were sitting on the floor with him, in a bare room. Sai Baba waved his right hand in the air and a small mound of vibuti appeared, which he divided up and gave to them.

As they went on talking, he again waved his hand in the air and produced a large gold ring which he presented to Dr Osis. Set into it was a portrait of Sai Baba on some enamelled material firmly encased by clasps.

When Sai Baba materialised these things, he did so after waving his hand in a characteristic way – small circular movements lasting for two or three seconds. The object then appeared in his hand. These effects are common with Sai Baba. Materialisation out of thin air is repeatedly described by visitors. Many report having seen him produce a variety of objects in this way and give them out as gifts.

Haraldsson and Osis had observed Sai Baba closely all the time. There was no obvious trickery in what they had seen. On the contrary the phenomena seemed genuine. But they needed to go further. They wanted to have Sai Baba participate in a more strictly controlled scientific experiment. It was while they were talking with him on this subject that he produced a third object, under circumstances which impressed them greatly.

> While we were arguing with Sai Baba about the value of science and controlled experimentation, he turned the discussion to his favourite topic, the spiritual life, which in his view should be as "grown together" with ordinary daily life as a "double rudraksha". We did not understand the term nor could the interpreter translate it. Sai Baba seemed to make several efforts to make its meaning clear to us until he gave in and with some signs of impatience closed his fist and waved his hand. He then opened his palm and showed us a double rudraksha, which we are told by Indian botanists is a rare specimen in nature like a twin orange or twin apple.

This incident very much impressed Haraldsson and Osis. As experienced and sceptical investigators of the paranormal, both were familiar with sleight of hand and the other arts of the magician – which are well-developed in India. Whilst the other objects could just conceivably have been produced in this way, the production of a perfect double rudraksha was another matter altogether. The subject of a double rudraksha had arisen spontaneously in conversation. That Sai Baba was able to produce a perfect specimen immediately was, in their opinion, quite remarkable. On subsequent investigation they found that the Botanical Survey of India had never actually seen a double rudraksha or had one in its collection. The only known examples of this freak of nature were small and malformed.

Very soon afterwards, the rudraksha – which is a small nut similar to an acorn – was involved in a further incident which pointed even more strongly to the paranormal as the only possible explanation.

> After we had admired the rudraksha, Sai Baba took it back in his hand and turning to Dr Haraldsson, said he wanted to give him a present. He enclosed the rudraksha between both his hands, blew on it, and opened his hands toward Dr Haraldsson. In his palm we again saw a double rudraksha, but it now had a golden ornamental shield on each side of it. These shields were about an inch in diameter and held together by golden chains on both sides. On top of the shield was a golden cross with a small ruby affixed to it. Behind the cross was an opening so that this ornament could be hung on a chain and worn around the neck. A goldsmith later examined this ornament and found that it contained 22-carat gold . . .
>
> A botanist's microscopic examination of the rudraksha showed it to be a genuine example of the species . . .

Haraldsson and Osis report that they watched Sai Baba's hands very closely during their interviews and never saw him take anything from his sleeves or reach toward his bushy hair, clothing or any other hiding place.

Sai Baba wears a one piece robe with sleeves that reach down to his wrists. When Haraldsson and Osis inspected the garment they found that it had no pockets and no sign of magician's paraphernalia having been attached. Furthermore, when Sai Baba produced vibuti there was never any sign of it on his clothing or on the inside of his sleeves.

Haraldsson and Osis continued to press Sai Baba to agree to a controlled scientific experiment, a request he consistently denied. However, in one session, the gold ring which Sai Baba had previously materialised and presented to Dr Osis did become the subject of a remarkable 'experiment'.

> This ring had a large enamelled picture in colour of Sai Baba encased in it. The picture was of oval shape, about 2cm long and 1cm wide, and was framed by the ring. The edges of the ring above and below the enamelled picture, together with four little notches that protruded over it from the circular golden frame, kept it fixed in the ring. Thus the picture was set firmly in the ring as if it and the ring were one solid article.
>
> In an interview during our second visit when we tried to persuade Sai Baba to participate in some controlled experi-

> ments, he seemed to become impatient and said to Dr Osis, "Look at your ring." The picture had disappeared from it. We looked for it on the floor, but no trace of it could be found. The frame and the notches that should have held the picture were undamaged; we examined them afterwards with a magnifying glass. For the picture to have fallen out of the frame, it would have been necessary to bend at least one of the notches and probably also to bend the frame at some point, but neither had been done. Another alternative would have been to break the picture in the ring so that it would fall into pieces.
>
> When Sai Baba made us aware of the picture's absence we were sitting on the floor about five or six feet away from him. We had not shaken hands when we entered the room and he did not reach out to us or touch us.
>
> As we sat cross-legged on the floor, Dr Osis had his hands on his thighs and Dr Haraldsson had noticed the picture in the ring during the interview and before this incident occurred . . . When the picture could not be found, Sai Baba somewhat teasingly remarked, "This was my experiment".

Sai Baba did not belittle science in his conversations with Haraldsson and Osis. But he said that he would not produce objects purely as a scientific experiment or for demonstration purposes to satisfy sceptics; he could only his use powers for the good and protection of his devotees. A head of state, he explained, has great powers – for example, to arrest people. But he cannot have someone arrested just to demonstrate his power.

Nonetheless, Sai Baba appeared to want to help the investigators as much as possible. In a session a few days later, he added a new twist to what he described as the 'ring experiment'. He began by asking Dr Osis if he wanted the picture back. Osis said that he did.

> "Do you want the same picture or a different one?", Sai Baba asked. "The same," Dr Osis replied. Sai Baba then closed his fingers around the ring in his palm, brought it about six inches from his mouth, blew at it lightly and then, stretching his hand toward us, opened it. In it was a ring. The enamelled picture was like the one that had been framed in the first ring; the ring itself, however, was different.

On their return to America, Haraldsson and Osis consulted

Douglas Henning, a celebrated professional magician living in New York, and they discussed their findings with him. Henning confirmed that, whilst it was possible to manifest objects by sleight of hand, it was beyond the skill of a magician to produce particular objects on demand. In particular, he found the 'picture in the ring' incident quite impossible to explain away as a magician's trick.

Haraldsson and Osis admit in the report that their observations were made under semi-spontaneous rather than strictly controlled conditions. However they make the following four points in relation to their investigation which make it very difficult to explain the phenomena away.

> 1. *We might have been in altered states of consciousness, like mass hypnosis, and have responded to skilful suggestion techniques by 'seeing' what was not there and overlooking actual, observable events. For example, the late Carl Vett explained his observations of the Indian rope trick in this way.* We are both psychologists and can state with confidence that we did not undergo any altered states during our interviews with Sai Baba. We were very much on our guard at all times. Moreover, the objects produced – the double rudraksha and the gold ring with the enamel picture – are still in our possession.
>
> 2. *The objects might have been provided by an accomplice in the interview room.* This is not possible because objects also appeared when we were alone in the room with Sai Baba. Moreover, the seating positions often excluded such a possibility . . .
>
> 3. *The interview room might have contained concealed devices which somehow ejected the objects we observed.* The room was barren of anything which could be so used. Sai Baba usually sat cross-legged on the concrete floor out of reach of any possible containers, such as a shopping bag or a windowsill, in which packages of vibuti or other small objects might be concealed. The place where he sat varied from interview to interview, and he was not positioned in one particular spot when the incidents occurred. He also produced objects outdoors and in a private room.
>
> 4. *Sai Baba might have concealed the objects on his person and produced them by sleight of hand.* We heard rumours about this possibility which suggested hiding places such as

> the sleeves of his robe, hidden pockets and even his hair. However, we found no one who could offer first-hand observations or who could name someone who had made first-hand observations supporting this hypothesis.

Haraldsson and Osis reported their conviction that the phenomena they observed were genuine. Among the reasons they cited in their report were:

> 1. Lengthy history without clear detection of fraud. According to those who have had a long association with Sai Baba, the seemingly paranormal flow of objects has lasted for some forty years, or since his childhood. Most of the persons we met who had had even just one meeting with him reported having observed some ostensible materialisation phenomena. We did not meet anyone who claimed personal observations indicative of Sai Baba having produced the objects by normal means.
>
> 2. Reports of the occurrence of other psi phenomena, such as ESP over distance, giving messages in dreams, healing, out-of-body projections collectively perceived, and psychokinesis of heavy objects.
>
> 3. Variety of circumstances in which objects appear: during private interviews, while travelling in a car, outdoors in the presence of crowds, in private homes, etc. Almost every time we saw Sai Baba, in public or in private, objects were produced.
>
> 4. Production of objects apparently in response to a specific situation or on the direct demand of the visitor. We encountered many witnesses who testified as to such occurrences: the appearance of statuettes of a deity, etc.
>
> 5. Reported production of large objects, e.g. a bowl the size of a dinner plate, and a basket of sweets twenty inches in diameter.
>
> 6. Production of objects at a distance from Sai Baba, such as prayer beads appearing on the windshield of a car being driven along an open country road, vibuti appearing on Sai Baba's pictures, fruit appearing directly in visitors' hands.

Since the publication of this 1977 report, Professor Haraldsson has continued to investigate the phenomena associated with Sai Baba. In an acclaimed book published in 1987, he documents scores of interviews with people who have encountered Sai Baba over the years. These eye-witness accounts tend to corroborate the earlier findings. They provide further evidence that the materialisation phenomena are real. In addition, they describe many other paranormal happenings. For example, Sai Baba is said to have prevented rain falling on large gatherings and to have fed a multitude of people from a small pot of hot food. He has also been seen to *teleport* – vanishing from amongst a group of people, he instantaneously appeared again some distance away. The sheer volume and richness of these incidents prompts Dr Osis to comment in a foreword to the book:

> The stories of Sai Baba's paranormal phenomena describe powers of a magnitude, variety and sustained frequency not encountered anywhere else in the modern world.

Sai Baba's reputation continues to draw to him large numbers of visitors from India and around the world. His 'miracles' have now been seen by hundreds of thousands of people. In over forty years, no one has been able to provide evidence of fraud, deception or magical tricks of any kind. On the contrary, almost everyone who visits Sai Baba comes away convinced that the phenomena associated with him are truly paranormal. No one who has spent any length of time with Sai Baba has any doubt that his 'miracles' are real.

The overall body of testimony is very convincing. It strongly suggests that Sai Baba has extraordinary powers – most frequently and obviously demonstrated in his materialisation of objects. He can make objects appear and disappear in ways that have no normal explanation. He uses no apparatus and can produce things instantly at will.

Some people might describe this power as 'mind over matter'. When asked by Haraldsson how he does it, Sai Baba replied, "Mental creation. I think, imagine, and then it is there".

Through the vortex, it is possible to put forward a picture of what is going on at a physical level. Transubstantiation is the key. Consider, for example, a gold ring in Sai Baba's hand. It would consist of billions of vortices of energy, arranged into atoms.

Imagine that Sai Baba could accelerate the movement in each and every vortex particle. The ring would disappear. Transubstantiated into super-energy, it would pass through the light-barrier into a super-physical realm. Leaving space and time, it would vanish from our world. In this dematerialisation, there would be no change in the arrangement of the particles: the form of the ring would be completely unaltered.

Sai Baba could bring the ring back by reversing the process. To re-materialise it, he would simply slow the vortex movement down again. As it returns through the light-barrier, the ring would reappear in our world. In the 'picture in the ring' incident, Sai Baba might have transubstantiated only the picture, leaving the ring itself unchanged.

But how could Sai Baba produce completely new objects out of thin air? Perhaps he has all sorts of objects *suspended* in a super-physical realm. They would be, as it were, 'stored on the shelf' outside our space and time. By bringing them back down through the light-barrier, he could cause them to appear in his hand or anywhere else. Sai Baba himself supports this idea when he talks about the 'Sai stores'.

It may be that Sai Baba can actually form things out of super-energy, using creative imagination. Some of these objects might be completely new. Others might be copies of something that already exists; he may be able to use an existing object as a *mould* for forming super-energy. In either case, he could keep the new objects in the 'Sai stores' or bring them immediately into our world.

Some of the objects Sai Baba produces may already exist in our world, but be 'brought in' from elsewhere. Perhaps he can dematerialise objects in one place, and then bring them back through the light-barrier in his own region of space and time. This would constitute an apport.

Sai Baba supports these ideas as well; of things he has produced, he has commented, "Sometimes it is created. Sometimes it is brought from somewhere else".

In short, Sai Baba might variously *suspend, create, replicate* and *transport* objects outside normal space and time prior to producing them. Between them, these various means can account for a great number of his purported miracles.

Take, for instance, the feeding of a great multitude from a small pot of food. The existing hot food in the pot could have been used as a template through which super-energy was continually 'extruded'; as it condensed into energy, a continuous supply of food could have been produced. This process, in which forms in our world are replicated, may also account for some of the miracles performed by Christ, two thousand years ago. For example, he could have used the loaves and fishes as templates for condensing super-energy into our world, in this way creating sufficient food to feed the five thousand.

The materialisations performed by Sai Baba appear to defy common sense. They are challenging to many people. However, by using the vortex – and the concepts of super-energy and transubstantiation – these apparent miracles can be accommodated within a rational framework. It becomes easier to accept these quite remarkable paranormal phenomena as reasonable.

It is repeating patterns that interest scientists, not unique events. If one human being possesses apparently miraculous powers, it may point to an ability that is latent in us all. Haraldsson and Osis asked Sai Baba how he could produce beautiful and precious objects out of nothing. Why could he do it and not they? He replied that we are all like matches – the difference is that he is on fire.

CHAPTER 5

Breaking out of space and time

An American photographer was in India and wanted to photograph Sai Baba with his sophisticated camera. However when he came to take the photographs, he was bitterly disappointed to find that he had insufficient film. The particular film he needed could not be obtained in that part of India. Sai Baba waved his hand in the air and manifested two rolls of the special film. The delighted American loaded his camera and proceeded to take the photographs of Sai Baba, who is unmistakable in appearance with his bushy hair and long flowing orange robes.

On his return to the USA, the photographer dropped the film into his usual supplier to be developed. When he collected the prints, the man behind the counter remarked on the pictures of Sai Baba, saying: "Why, that man was in here a few weeks ago and bought two rolls of film".

There are numerous accounts of Sai Baba visiting people in one place when it is known that he is somewhere else. This extraordinary ability to be in two places at the same time is known as bilocation. Bilocation is by no means unique to Sai Baba. Known in India as a *siddhi*, it is one of a number of remarkable powers traditionally ascribed to advanced yogis.

The famous 20th century yogi, Paramahansa Yogananda (1883-1952), first encountered the power of bilocation at the age of twelve. This incident impressed him deeply, and is described in his book *The Autobiography of a Yogi*. Yogananda was running an errand for his father; he had been sent into the local town of Benares to deliver a letter. His father had mislaid the address, so he sent the boy instead to a certain Swami Pranabananda who could forward on the letter.

When Yogananda arrived at the Swami's home the front door was open. The boy entered to find a rather stout man in a loin-

Figure 11. Paramahansa Yogananda

cloth meditating. No warning had been given that Yogananda was coming, but it was immediately clear that he was expected. Before Yogananda could even introduce himself, the swami said, "Are you Bhagabati's son? Of course I will locate your father's friend for you".

The swami then closed his eyes and went back into meditation. Young Yogananda shuffled about awkwardly in the silence, not knowing what to do or say.

After a while, Swami Pranabananda opened his eyes and smiled at Yogananda. "Little sir", he said, "don't get worried. The man you wish to see will be with you in half an hour". With that the swami once more resumed his meditation. The minutes ticked by. Yogananda glanced at his watch now and again, but most of the time he kept his eyes on the yogi.

After half an hour had passed, the swami aroused himself and announced that the man was nearing the door. Moments later, there were footsteps on the stairs. A man entered and went up to Yogananda.

"Are you Bhagabati's son who is waiting for me?", he asked. "Half an hour ago, Swami Pranabananda approached me as I was bathing in the Ganges.

I don't know how he knew I was there. He said you were waiting to see me at his apartment and asked me to return there with him. He grasped me by the hand and said it was a half-hour walk. He then announced that he had other business to attend to, left me and melted away into the crowd."

Yogananda found it hard to believe what the man was saying. "Why", he exclaimed, "Swami Pranabananda has not left my sight for a moment since I first came about an hour ago!"

Bilocation is at the limit of what many people can believe. However there are numerous accounts of this extraordinary phenomenon down through the ages. The Greek sage Pythagoras, reputed to have established esoteric mystery schools, is said to have bilocated on at least one occasion.

According to his biographer Iamblicus, Pythagoras once taught on the same day in two places: one on the island of Sicily, and the other on the Italian mainland, normally many days journey away.

Even in this century, two well-known mystics – Therese Neumann and Padra Pio – are said to have bilocated. Padre Pio

(1887-1968) was an Italian monk famous for his paranormal gifts – including telepathy, miraculous healing, and the stigmata. He first experienced bilocation in January 1905; while in the choir of his seminary in Italy, he suddenly found himself transported into the midst of a wealthy household in a remote city. The family there was in crisis; the wife was giving birth whilst her husband was dying. Padre Pio was able to help them, and subsequently played a vital role in the child's adult life.

Those who bilocate usually have a range of other paranormal powers as well. In the case of Sai Baba, the most significant of these is of course materialisation, which we have explained in terms of transubstantiation.

Some people believe that bilocation is not a physical event; they attribute it to some form of out-of-the-body projection or apparition. However, there is evidence that a real body can exist simultaneously in two places. In the examples we have quoted, Swami Pranabananda shook hands with a man by the Ganges, Padre Pio spent several hours in physical contact with the distressed family, and Sai Baba walked into an American photographic shop to buy two rolls of film.

Bilocation can be explained as a real, physical event in terms of transubstantiation.

If Sai Baba can transubstantiate inanimate objects, perhaps he could do the same thing with his own body. Imagine that he could take his body at will through the light-barrier. Leaving our space and time in one place, Sai Baba could re-enter it at another. He could pass through the light-barrier in India and return through it in America. Sai Baba could spend as long as he liked there, visiting photographic shops and buying rolls of film. He could then reverse the process and return, having travelled in and out of space and time rather than through it.

What if he chose to return to the precise point in space, in India, from which he departed? What if he could enter into the exact moment of time at which he left? To the people in India, it would be as if he had never left their presence. Occurring in less than the twinkling of an eye, it would seem as if nothing had happened.

The swami in Yogananda's story could have followed the same procedure. Leaving his room through a 'door' in space-time, rather than through the door in his wall, he could have gone to collect the man from the Ganges. To young Yogananda, it would not be apparent that he had ever left his posture of meditation.

Linking bilocation with the ability to make objects appear and disappear means that we only need to assume one miraculous power to account for both phenomena. This is the power of transubstantiation, the ability to raise the speed of energy, in matter, beyond that of light. By this means, a person could pass through the light-barrier in body, leaving one place in our world to appear instantaneously somewhere else; a master of this process could appear and disappear at will, wherever and whenever he chose.

There is an alternative explanation – also involving transubstantiation – which does not require the body to move. It could be that what appears in bilocation is a duplicate body. The original body might be used as a 'template' to form a precise replica out of super-energy. It would then be this *doppel-ganger* that materialises elsewhere. The bilocation would still be a physical event, in which a real body exists in two places at the same time. But it would be only the consciousness of the person, moving freely from one body to another, that stepped in and out of space-time.

The powers of *clairvoyance* and *precognition* could find their explanation in the ability of some gifted individuals to probe beyond the light-barrier in consciousness only. Re-entering space-time at remote points in mind rather than in body, these individuals could catch a glimpse of the future and faraway places.

Before going any further in explaining the paranormal using these ideas, we need to consider the nature of space and time. The vortex offers a new explanation for what space is. It also enables us to understand the relationship between matter, space and time. Not only matter, but also space and time, can be seen as aspects of the vortex.

Consider the vortex of energy forming matter. As the vortex extends out, the energy would get thinner. Stretching over an ever-increasing area, it would rapidly get thinner and thinner. But even at great distances from the centre of the vortex, though ever-increasing area, it would rapidly get thinner and thinner. But even at great distances from the centre of the vortex, though the intensity would be infinitesimal, the vortex energy would still be there. The apparent void of space is actually very thin matter.

By the same token, it could be said that matter is very dense space. In a nutshell, matter and space are one and the same thing – they are two aspects of the same vortex of energy. What we think of as a particle of matter is merely the dense centre of an extended vortex of energy.

We only perceive matter and space as different because of our senses. All our senses are limited. Our awareness of all forms of energy is constrained within certain bands by our *thresholds of perception*. Our eyes respond to light. But light is only a narrow band of the spectrum; we are blind, for example, to infra-red and ultra-violet. It is the same with sound; we can only perceive sound within certain limits. The human ear only detects sound above a certain threshold; very weak sound vibrations are inaudible to us. Our perception of pitch is also restricted. Dogs can hear high frequency whistles to which our ears are deaf; the sound energy is there, but we are not aware of it.

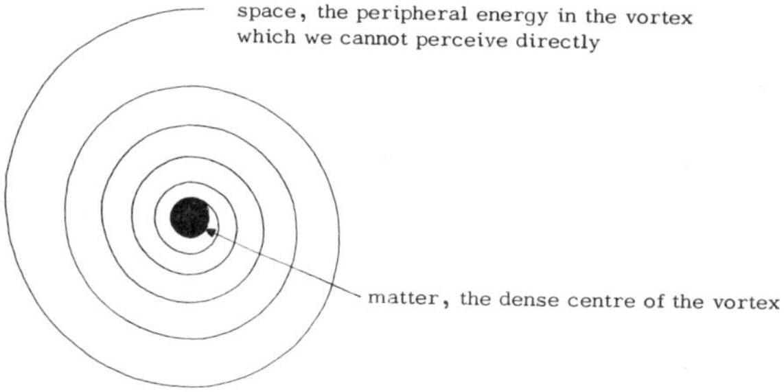

Figure 12. Matter and space are merely two different aspects of the vortex of energy

It is obvious that our awareness of energy in the vortex would also be limited by our senses. The sparse energy extending in the vortex, beyond our direct perception, would appear to us to be 'empty space'. Whereas it would seem to be nothing but a void, this extending energy would be very real – as real as matter itself.

This account of space begins to explain the puzzling phenomenon of action-at-a-distance. In both electric charge and magnetism, one particle acts on another without touching it. Separate bits of matter seem to attract or repel each across apparently empty space.

These effects are easy to understand if each particle is actually an extended vortex of energy. The vortex could extend over a vast distance, but the energy would quickly become so sparse that we are not aware of it. This energy extending out invisibly from the particle would overlap – and interact with – the energy of other vortices to create such effects as electric charge and magnetism.

In this picture, space is something real, as real as matter, and action-at-a-distance is an illusion, created by the limitations of

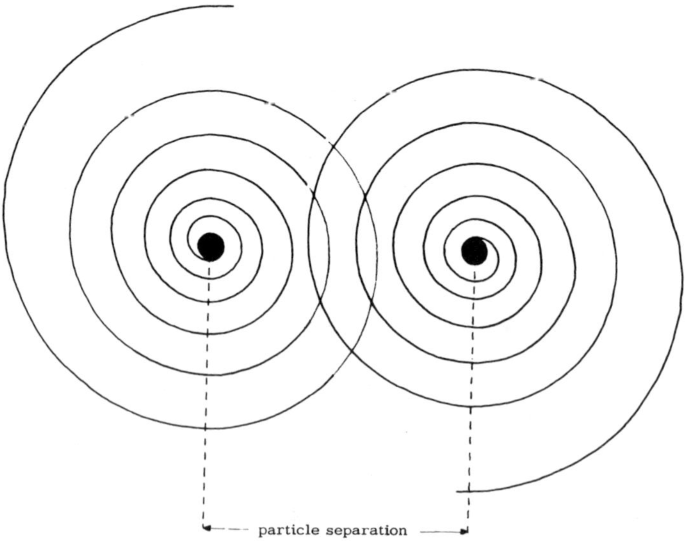

Figure 13. As vortices overlap, they interact across apparently empty space

our senses. Matter is the dense central region of the vortex, which we can detect with our senses. Space has its origin in the thin, peripheral regions of the vortex: here the energy is below the threshold of our perception. 'Space' transmits the intrinsically dynamic nature of matter out into the void beyond the apparent surface. But matter has no real boundary: its 'surface' is subjective rather than objective – corresponding to the lowest intensity of vortex energy that we can perceive.

We experience everyday matter as substantial because it represents a high concentration of energy. In bodies of matter, billions of vortices are packed together in atoms and molecules, bound tightly together. The surface of a solid or liquid marks a sudden increase in the number of vortices – a vast increase in the intensity of vortex energy. This sudden high concentration of energy and binding is what our senses detect as matter. Objects appear to have boundaries. But this is an illusion. It is simply that our senses are incapable of detecting the sparse energy spreading out in all directions.

Imagine a woman wearing a perfume. Around her, the scent is concentrated so that close to her we can smell it. Further away, the scent disperses into the atmosphere and we no longer perceive it. In short, as it expands, the bubble of scent becomes too dilute for us to be aware of it. We could picture space as a similar 'bubble' of energy surrounding matter. Each particle of matter would be surrounded by a bubble of space emanating from it.

Space would form like foam as bubbles merged from billions of particles. The space of the physical universe would be the addition of all the bubbles reaching out from each and every particle of matter in existence. The loss of a single particle would lead to the loss of the bubble of space attached to it. If it were possible to destroy every particle of matter in the universe, then space would completely disappear.

This new picture of space is very different from that held by most people. For most of us, the word space conjures up the idea of nothingness; an absolute void in which matter is free to move. We think of it, not as something real, but as the emptiness left behind when everything else is removed. This idea of space is so fundamental that few of us can imagine it any other way.

This traditional picture of space can be traced back to the Greeks. At the dawn of modern science, two thousand years later, it was endorsed by Sir Isaac Newton. Newton envisaged space as an absolute void, existing independently of anything else.

It was not until the turn of the 20th century that Newton's picture of space was seriously challenged. In his theory of Relativity, Einstein shook the idea of absolute space to pieces. Einstein was only five years old when he began to think about space. It was a childhood experience which ultimately led to his theories of Relativity and to his becoming the most celebrated scientist in the world. Young Albert was ill and had to spend a couple of days in bed.

When he was feeling better, his father gave him a compass. The boy spent a day playing with it. He was fascinated by the fact that the needle kept pointing in the same direction, regardless of how he moved the compass. He knew nothing of the earth's magnetic field; he simply assumed that space itself was holding the needle as the compass moved. In his youthful, questioning mind he concluded that space had to have some real substance to it in order to hold the needle. His assumption that space was holding the compass needle was wrong. However, this mistake marked a turning point in human history. Einstein's conviction that space was not just a void never left him.

Many years later, Einstein came to view both space and time as in some way inextricably linked with matter. When asked to explain his theory of Relativity in a couple of sentences, his reply in a nutshell was:

> Remove matter from the universe and you also remove space and time.

In this cryptic remark, Einstein was saying that space and time do not exist independently of matter, but are somehow connected to it. If, when going, matter takes space with it, space cannot be an emptiness that is left behind when matter is gone. In some way, when matter is removed, space and time are also removed with it.

Since Einstein, most scientists have accepted the extraordinary ideas in the theories of Relativity. Space-time is curved and this effect is somehow related to matter. But precisely what space is, and how matter can influence it, has remained an enigma.

The vortex, for the first time, offers a straightforward picture of space which makes it easy to see what space is and how it is related to matter. The idea that space is linked to matter is no longer a puzzle: the 'bubble' model for space makes it obvious that, if you remove matter from the universe, you also remove space.

Just as the vortex creates space and matter, so it can be seen as creating time. Einstein believed that, in the absence of matter, there would be no space and no time either. He saw time and space as being inextricably linked, with time as a fourth dimension. We can see, through the vortex, why time is linked to matter.

Time is established by a repeating sequence of events. Take our familiar measures of time. The year is set up by the movement of the Earth round the sun; the day is set up by the spin on the Earth on its axis. These are regular repeating processes. In our world, one sequence of processes is linked to another. All physical, chemical and biological changes take their 'beat' from other more fundamental regular processes; one regular, repeating process creates 'intervals' of time relative to which other sets of changes occur.

Is there some fundamental process in the universe on which all other measures of time could be built? Spin in the vortex could well be this ultimate process. The vortex may be acting as a primordial clock – ticking out the intervals of time on which all other sub-atomic and cosmic processes depend. The vortex could be pictured as a 'flywheel' marking out time – the ultimate atomic clock at the heart of all matter.

In this new picture, both time and space have a physical reality. Time flows from movement in the vortex and space is an extension of the vortex form. Imagine the vortex as a whirlpool in a river. Its form is created by swirling water. The form of the whirlpool would represent matter and space. The swirl of the water would represent time.

This account of space and time casts new light on Relativity. For example, curved space-time is fundamental to Relativity. The vortex picture shows very clearly how space-time can be

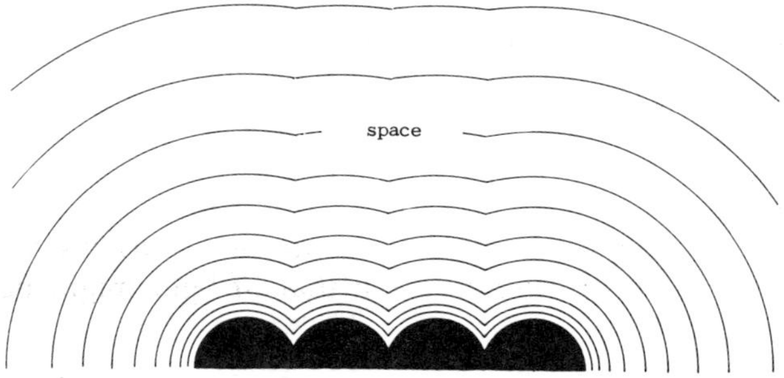

Figure 14. The space around an object is an extended field of energy with the same 'shape' as the matter

curved; if space is a bubble around matter, it would obviously take on the shape of the matter. The space bubble extending from a heavenly body, such as the sun, would necessarily be an extension of the spherical shape of the sun.

Before Einstein, space and time were each regarded as an endless continuum in which events took place. Newton taught that space and time were both absolute, existing quite independently of each other or anything else. Einstein showed, by contrast, that space and time are not fundamental and absolute, but closely related to each other and dependent on the the speed of light.

The vortex shows how space, time and matter all arise from the vortex of energy; as such they are inextricably linked – they are simply different aspects of a single underlying reality. If the speed of movement in the vortex is the speed of light, then it is obvious why space, time and matter are all linked, and relative to the speed of light.

Einstein regarded the speed of light as the limit of our world. We have suggested that the speed of light is not an absolute boundary – but rather the dividing line between physical and super-physical reality. These two realities differ in substance because movement is entirely relative. Movement in one vortex creates the space and time in which another can exist and move. They are all totally interdependent; they exist only in relation to each other. In transubstantiation, the movement in the vortex is speeded up. As it exceeds the speed of light, the particle ceases to have any relationship to the other particles left behind. In effect, it leaves their physical space and time.

Breaking out of space and time by transubstantiation would open up entirely new possibilities for travel. In our everyday experience, we travel *through* space and time. Via transubstantiation, bodies could move *in and out* of space-time, passing through the light-barrier. By this means, journeys at speeds which appear to be greater than that of light might be a real possibility.

CHAPTER 6

UFOs Explained

"Beam me up Scotty", orders Captain Kirk. The next instant, he vanishes off the surface of some alien planet to reappear aboard the Starship Enterprise.

An old-fashioned police telephone box dematerialises; with its characteristic sound, the 'Tardis' vanishes to transport the time lord, Dr Who, through a space-time tunnel from one place and age in the universe to another.

Television series such as 'Startrek' and 'Dr Who' have popularised many science fiction ideas. In science fiction, spacecraft vanish instantly as they leave to warp their way through space and time. Such ideas may seem fanciful, but history has shown that science fiction often anticipates fact.

Through the vortex, we can offer a framework for bringing these science fiction ideas into the realm of reality. If it were possible to move *in* and *out* of space and time, spacecraft could pass from one star system to another without journeying *through* space or time. Passing through the light-barrier via transubstantiation, a traveller could leave space and time to re-enter the universe at any place or time that he or she chose. With this form of *inter-space* travel, time and distance would be no obstacle. By this means of transcending space and time, the mysteries of UFOs could be explained.

UFOs have excited the imagination of many people. The number of UFO sightings is enormous. These strange craft became known as flying saucers from one of the first UFO sightings to hit the headlines in America.

On June 24th, 1947 an American businessman, Kenneth Arnold, was flying his own light aircraft in Washington State. The weather was clear and fine; as Arnold subsequently reported, *"flying was a real pleasure."* Suddenly, he was startled by a bright light. Then he noticed a row of strange craft flying at about 10,000 feet, approaching from the north. To begin with, he thought they were aircraft. But then Arnold noticed, to his amazement, that they were shaped like saucers and were flying without tails, wings or apparent engines.

As they banked, sunlight was reflected off their metallic hulls. This was the bright light that had first startled him.

Arnold's story was reported in the newspapers and caused a sensation. From his description of these strange craft, the term *flying saucers* was born.

Arnold's observation of unidentified flying objects was not the first. Throughout history people have reported sightings of strange objects in the sky. In the Second World War, allied pilots christened them *"foo fighters"*.

One bomber pilot described his encounters with foo fighters over Germany in these terms: *"They looked something like crystal balls flying in formation alongside our aircraft but never closer than about 300 feet. After a while they would peel off and vanish."*

Since the war, the number of UFO sightings has escalated dramatically. UFOs have been seen by people from all walks of life. However it is mostly reports reports from pilots, air force and airline officers that have been taken seriously enough to be thoroughly investigated. The following descriptions, taken from *The UFO Phenomenon* by Johannes von Buttlar, are typical examples of what air forces and airlines have had to contend with.

On January 7th, 1948 a silvery disc about 300 feet in diameter was seen above Louisville, Kentucky. Pilots Hammonds, Clement and Mantell were scrambled from a nearby air base in pursuit. Just after 3pm Mantell reported a large disc, 80 yards in diameter. The upper surface had a ring and a dome and it was turning fantastically fast, apparently round a central vertical axis.

Mantell was flying at 31,500 feet.

There was feverish activity in the control tower as the radar locked onto the disc. The fighters were chasing it. Mantell came in again to say that he was flying twice as fast and overtaking the craft. He said it had a metallic gleam but was shrouded in yellowish light which changed to become reddish-orange. He then reported that the disc was speeding up. It was trying to escape, climbing at about forty-five degrees.

The two other pilots gave up the chase but Mantell continued in hot pursuit. He came in again. His last words were, " *The thing's gigantic. It's flying unbelievably fast. I can see windows. Now . . .*"

At about 4pm a search party found the wreckage of Mantell's plane scattered over an area a mile across. When they found the pilot's body, his watch had stopped at 15:18.

This event caused a sensation. The sighting of a strange object in the sky was unusual. But air force fighters chasing a huge UFO in broad daylight was outrageous. When one of the fighters almost made contact and then crashed as a result, the papers had a field-day.

UFO reports began to come in thick and fast. Even more dramatic incidents soon followed, some involving both civil and military aircraft.

It was just before midnight on July 19th, 1952. To traffic controllers at the Washington National Airport, it had been a quiet and uneventful evening.

Suddenly, their peace was shattered. A whole formation of UFOs erupted without warning onto their radar screens. Flight controllers watched in amazement.

At first, the UFOs were moving slowly, but then they took off at fantastic speed. Crews of several airlines began to report the objects crossing their flight paths – their accounts subsequently being confirmed by eye-witnesses on the ground. Then, as mysteriously as the discs had appeared, they vanished again.

Suddenly the UFOs reappeared. F-94 fighters were scrambled. But as soon as the jets intercepted them, the UFOs melted away.

But they hadn't gone. Very quickly, they were back again. Two flew down the restricted corridor over the White House. A third circled above Capitol Hill. In the course of the night, the UFOs appeared again and again, flashing multi-coloured lights, but each time the fighters approached them they vanished.

Americans began to speculate that UFOs were a new Russian secret weapon. However, UFOs were also appearing over the USSR.

In the same summer of 1952, a gigantic cigar-shaped object,

at least 2,500 feet long, appeared over the Russian town of Voronezh. Slowly, it descended to about 6,000 feet, where it remained motionless for some time. Thousands of people saw it and many were panic-stricken.

Suddenly the craft vanished. Minutes later, two fighters appeared in the sky. They soon left, reporting that nothing was there.

However, immediately they had gone, the vast UFO reappeared again in the precise place from which it had vanished. An orange ray of light shone out from one end. It then rose vertically into the air, and without a sound, shot off at great speed.

People who haven't seen a UFO tend to dismiss them as figments of imagination. However, the authorities have been obliged to take them very seriously.

In 1960 an American television documentary surveyed the research into UFOs since the war. The programme included an official communique from the US Defence Department stating that the Pentagon accepted the reality of UFOs and the possibility that they were under intelligent direction. The Pentagon was reported to have concluded that there was no earthly explanation for these strange craft or the advanced technology that they demonstrated.

Von Buttlar quotes a number of senior air force officers who support the reality of UFO phenomena. Lieutenant-General Nathan F. Twining, as Commander-in-Chief of the US Air Material Command, made an official report on UFOs to the American government in which he emphasised that their sightings should not be dismissed as visionary or fictitious. In England, Air Chief Marshal Lord Dowding said, "*The existence of these machines is proved*".

Captain Ruppelt, an official investigator of these phenomena for the US Air Force, had the following to say to those who doubt the existence of UFOs:

> What constitutes proof? Does a UFO have to land at the River Entrance to the Pentagon, near the Joint Chiefs of Staff offices? Or is it proof when a ground radar station detects a UFO, sends a jet to intercept it, the jet pilot sees it, and locks on with his radar, only to have the UFO streak

> away at phenomenal speed? Is it proof when a jet pilot fires at a UFO and sticks to his story even under the threat of court-martial. Does this constitute proof?

There are films of UFOs and a host of photographs. Witnesses have included pilots, astronauts, scientists and statesmen – even a former president of the United States. American astronauts have reported seeing UFOs on three separate occasions and on one of them the strange craft was photographed. The most dramatic space encounter occurred on September 14th, 1969. The Apollo XII astronauts, Conrad, Gordon and Bean were on the second mission to the moon. They reported back to mission control in Houston that two UFOs were flying alongside and that they appeared to be signalling to the capsule.

The real problem with UFOs is not a shortage of evidence but rather the absence of any scientific explanation for their existence and behaviour. It is difficult if not impossible to accommodate UFOs in existing scientific thinking. As a result it is tempting to reject the evidence and dismiss the idea of UFOs out of hand.

There are reports of mysterious flying objects going right back into prehistory. In his book *Chariots of the Gods?* Erich Von Danikeñ popularised the idea that prehistorical UFO sightings and encounters gave rise to many of man's ideas about the gods. He claimed that both historical and contemporary UFO sightings could be explained in terms of visits from extraterrestrials.

Many scientists would admit that there may be intelligent life elsewhere in the universe. They would also agree that with so many billions of stars in our galaxy, and millions of other galaxies, there might well be civilisations with technologies far in advance of our own. The astronomer Carl Sagan is an enthusiastic proponent of the possibility of extraterrestrial civilisations. In his book *The Cosmic Connection* he says:

> Civilisations hundreds or thousands of millions of years beyond us should have science and technologies so far beyond our present capabilities as to be indistinguishable from magic. It is not that what they do violates the laws of physics; it is that we do not understand how they are able to use the laws of physics to do what they do.

However, Sagan dismisses the possibility that extraterrestrials could ever visit us. Estimating that there are 10,000 million planets worth investigating in our galaxy alone, he considers that visiting them all would be an insuperable task for a civilisation searching space for intelligent life.

In addition, Von Daniken's notion that such visitors could travel *through* space from other star systems in conventional ways is untenable. The problem lies in the sheer vastness of space. Scientists generally agree that it would be physically impossible for craft to travel *through* space from one inhabited planet in the universe to another. Even if craft were travelling at very high speeds, they would take centuries to get here.

Von Daniken suggested that, if UFOs were able to achieve speeds near to that of light, they could take advantage of the slowing of time predicted by the theory of relativity. However, even with this suggestion, interstellar travel would still be unrealistic.

Accelerating a craft to speeds near that of light would require vast amounts of energy. Approaching the speed of light, the craft would grow more massive as it moved faster, so that the energy required for further acceleration would increase exponentially. Furthermore, if a craft achieved these high speeds, the energy required to slow it down or change direction would be enormous.

Another aspect of UFO observations that scientists find impossible to explain is the fact that these strange craft appear to materialise and dematerialise. It is this bewildering behaviour of UFOs that led the astrophysicist Dr Jacques Vallee to comment:

> The things we call unidentified flying objects are neither objects nor flying. They can dematerialise, as some recent photographs show, and they violate the laws of motion as we know them.

Physics has no way of explaining the mysterious materialisations and dematerialisations of UFOs. However, in the light of the vortex, it is precisely this behaviour which provides the clue to understanding them. It is the very fact that UFOs often appear and disappear instantly which could lead to an explanation of how they get here.

The inexplicable appearance and disappearance of UFOs suggests that they are moving *in and out* of space and time rather than *through* it. It points to the possibility that the occupants of UFOs have mastered transubstantiation, enabling them to take the matter in their craft through the light-barrier. If this is so, they would be able to vanish out of the space and time of their home planet in some distant star system. Then, decelerating through the light-barrier, they could enter the space and time of our planet – to suddenly and mysteriously appear out of nowhere.

It is tempting, in our technological age, to imagine that the occupants of UFOs have mastered a technology that enables them to transubstantiate matter. This may be so. Alternatively, they may be masters of some power similar to that exhibited by yogis, saints and mystics. If Sai Baba can make objects materialise and dematerialise, perhaps the occupants of UFOs can do the same with their craft. Apollonius, Christ and Mohammed, Padre Pio, Therese Neumann and Swami Pranabananda appear to have had the ability to travel in and out of space and time. Maybe there are whole civilisations on distant planets who can do the same.

It may be that, in other parts of the physical universe, intelligent beings regularly translocate by this means. For them, cars, planes and trains would not be necessary. They could just disappear in one place and turn up in another. Perhaps, like Sai Baba, they just imagine things into reality. They 'think' themselves into another place and there they instantly are.

It could be that UFOs are peopled by intelligent beings so advanced that they can project themselves in and out of space and time by an act of pure will. Alternatively, it may be that the power of their mind is somehow amplified, acting in concert with a very advanced technology. Perhaps the UFO craft carry these technological systems. On Earth, those who possess the power of translocation do not depend on vehicles. However to transport a whole team of personnel and their equipment may be beyond the power of a single unaided mind. Some technology for harnessing, amplifying and focusing the mind very precisely may be required.

There is another reason why extraterrestrials might need a UFO craft. As soon as they transubstantiated into matter, they would enter an alien atmosphere. They would possibly need a familiar atmosphere and other life-support systems, which a craft could supply. The craft might also have systems to counteract the force of gravity, enabling it to hover above the surface of a planet. If gravity has something to do with the vortex, this may be why UFOs are often seen with spinning domes.

Many of the mysteries of UFOs can be explained by the vortex. If they are extraterrestrial in origin, the key mystery is how they could reach us across the vast expanses of space. But this problem dissolves if UFOs are actually translocating outside space and time. Then take the way these craft suddenly appear and disappear. This need no longer be a puzzle, if they are entering and leaving our space-time through the light-barrier.

If this understanding of the UFO phenomenon is correct, then it implies god-like powers: the same power used by Sai Baba today and Jesus Christ two thousand years ago. We humans, with our infant science, have power only over the forms of energy. The more advanced science available to the occupants of UFOs would appear to confer power over the substance of energy. Whether the occupants of UFOs have developed a technology of transubstantiation or whether they achieve it purely by an immense act of will is an open question. In either case, if this power is the power of the gods, then it would have been entirely appropriate for Von Danikeñ to describe UFOs as 'chariots of the gods'.

CHAPTER 7

Dimension of the Gods

Throughout history, in all cultures, there have been legends of other realms. People have always spoken of gods and other supernatural beings, existing in some unearthly dimension. Folklore of domains beyond death, populated by gods, is as old as man. Traditionally, people looked to temples and churches, oracles and priests for knowledge of other-worldly realities. Today, the search for the supernatural has extended beyond religion. Some seek out guidance channelled from beings in other dimensions. Others visit clairvoyants and psychics who claim to be in touch with realms beyond the physical. Is it all just a figment of the imagination?

Do these supernatural realms and other dimensions really exist? Or are they, as many people suppose, a residue of primitive belief – fairy-tales perpetuated in folklore and religion. Is there some uniform hallucination to which people everywhere are prone? Are realms of thc supernatural just a fantasy produced by the human psyche? Or are they for real?

Since time immemorial, man has stepped out into the night and gazed into the starry sky with awe. The heavens were full of drama. In the sky, mysterious forces seemed to be at battle. It was natural for people to look upwards for superior powers. In the age of moon-shots and radio telescopes, no one seriously supposes that heavenly realms exist in outer space. But if heaven is not 'up there' somewhere, out in space, where could it be? Is the supposed 'heavenly realm' of the gods a real part of the universe or not?

The first thing to be clear about is the meaning of the word 'universe' itself. Most people think of the universe in terms of planets, stars and galaxies. This is the physical universe we are familiar with, the universe of matter and light.

But is this all there is? Is there nothing more than matter and light? Is the universe restricted to what we can detect with our scientific instruments and observe with our senses? Science has probed deeply into the material universe. But could this be only the beginning? Could our universe of matter and light be but a part of something much greater?

The word 'universe' means all existing things. It must encompass the totality of energy in existence. In previous chapters, we have talked about super-energy. We have speculated that forms of energy can exist beyond matter and light. If this is so, there may be much more to the universe than we think. There could be whole realms of super-energy. Existing beyond the light-barrier, they would form a reality beyond our perception.

The physical universe might be only a small part of the whole. It may not be restricted to the world that we see with our senses – and observe scientifically through telescope and microscope. The world from minute atom to mighty galaxy might be merely a part of a much greater universe of energy. The universe might be vaster by far than science has previously allowed. The heavenly realms, reputed domain of the gods, may be real, a parallel reality created out of super-energy.

In this super-physical reality, there could be vortices of super-energy, akin to particles of matter. There could be waves of super-energy, akin to light. Together, they could set up a whole *super-physical* world. Just as our world and the things within it are forms of energy, so this other reality would consist of forms of super-energy. Would this other reality be much like ours? Not necessarily. It might contain other primordial forms, apart from the vortex and wave. Dynamic forms of super-energy beyond our wildest imaginings might exist in the super-physical world.

It is obvious that we could not travel to the super-physical realm through space and time. The fabric of our space and time is created by the vortex. It does not reach into the higher realm. The super-physical realms are not 'up there' somewhere.

These realms would be beyond our space and time. In our world, each vortex creates a bubble of space and time. A vortex of super-energy would create a separate bubble of space and time, beyond the light-barrier. There could be countless vortices beyond the light-barrier, creating countless bubbles. Merging together like foam, they would set up an entire space-time realm quite distinct from our own.

Energy creates one space-time realm. Super-energy creates another. The fabric of space and time exists within each realm – there is no basis for space and time to exist between them. The distinct realms of energy and super-energy could not possibly be separated by space and time. They would occur in a single 'here and now'. They would exist independently, but be completely coincident. They could be described as *interpenetrating* one another.

Our realm is formed out of movement at the speed of light. This movement, in vortex and wave, builds our physical world of matter and light. In the physical universe, everything is relative to the speed of light. It could be described as the *critical* speed of our world.

A realm of super-energy would have its own critical speed, say, for example, twice the speed of light. It is easy to imagine several such realms of super-energy, each built out of a different, successively higher speed. There could be many super-physical realms in the universe. Each realm would have its own space and time, and would represent a distinct *plane* or *level* of reality.

Just as everything in our world is relative to the speed of light, so each higher realm would be governed by its own critical speed. In the same way that the light-barrier is the frontier of the physical universe, each critical speed would form a boundary between one realm and the next.

This series of realms in the universe could be likened to a set of Russian dolls. In a set of Russian dolls, each smaller, inner doll is nested within a larger, outer one. The distinct realms of the universe would be related in a similar way. The higher realms would embrace the lower realms – because greater speeds 'contain' all lesser speeds. As all speeds are centred on a common point of zero, we might picture the realms as concentric nested spheres.

The inner spheres would represent the lower, slower realms and the outer spheres the higher, faster realms. This picture of the universe portrays how the realms embrace each other, and shows how each greater realm interpenetrates all the lesser ones.

The successive critical speeds might well be arranged in a

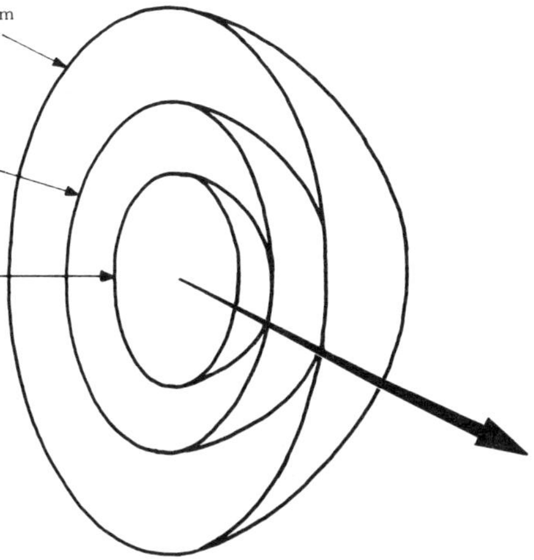

Figure 15. The different realms of the universe can be represented as a series of concentric spheres. Each successively higher realm includes all the lower ones.

simple ascending order. For example: physical realm = the speed of light, first super-physical realm = 2 x speed of light, second non-physical realm = 3 x speed of light, and so on. Such an ascending series would be like a harmonic scale. These ascending realms of energy in the universe would then give a real meaning to the idea of the 'harmony of the spheres' suggested by Pythagoras.

Imagine that the critical speed in the first higher realm is twice that of light. All forms of energy with speeds at or below that value would be part of it. It follows that our physical universe would fall within this higher realm – our world would be part of the overall domain of super-energy. Our reality would be a subset of the higher realms, and our space and time would be enclosed by the space and time created by super-energy.

If there are higher realms than ours, are there lower ones? The answer would seem to be no. The evidence is that our world is the lowest realm of energy in the universe.

The critical speed of our realm is the speed of light. Within our world, all forms of energy with speeds at or below the speed of light can be detected and measured scientifically. If a realm of *sub-energy* existed, it would be part of our world and we could be aware of it.

Another way to picture the form of the universe is to imagine a box of matches in a room. The matchbox would represent the lesser, inner realm of energy. The room would correspond to the greater, outer realm of super-energy.

The box is part of the room. It fits into the room. However, the room isn't part of the matchbox; the room can't be fitted inside the box! We can locate the matchbox in the room; we can say where it is in the room. But to ask where the room is in the matchbox is meaningless.

We could extend the matchbox analogy to consider how the room is contained in a house and the house in a town. Moving from box, to room, to house, and into the town we would enter ever-increasing realms of experience.

It is easy to see from this analogy how inhabitants of one realm might have only limited access to adjacent realms. Imagine people confined to one room of the house. They would be able to peer through the keyhole and catch a glimpse of what is happening elsewhere in the house. Through the window, they might be able to gain an impression of the world outside. But, confined to one room, they would have no real experience of the rest of the house, let alone the town. Knowledge of the outside world would be very sketchy. There would be much speculation about these mysterious other places and their possible inhabitants. Some people might even deny that they existed, and put it all down to illusion or wishful thinking.

This account begins to explain many of the traditional ideas about the supernatural. It shows how supernatural beings could exist in their own realms of space and time, interpenetrating our world. They could be all around us without our being aware of them through scientific instruments or any of the five normal human senses. It would be as if we were matches in the matchbox, unaware of the room or its occupants.

Many psychic powers could find their explanation in the ability of some individuals to probe with their consciousness through the light-barrier into the higher realms. Some people with 'psychic faculties' claim to be aware of supernatural beings and even to commune with them. With this so-called 'sixth sense', they appear to be able to transcend normal space and time and see into these other realms. To such people, the walls of the matchbox are transparent; they can see out.

But is there any way we could actually move from one realm of the universe to another? Could we move from matchbox to room, from the room into the house? We move in dimensions. When we move about, we travel in the three dimensions of space. In our journey from cradle to grave, we travel in the fourth dimension, of time.

The different realms of the universe would have to be separated from one another by yet a further dimension: this would be a fifth dimension.

The fifth dimension would be the cardinal dimension. It would be the dimension of speed itself. Linking one critical speed with another, it would be the dimension connecting all the distinct realms of energy in the universe.

The fifth dimension would be quite different from the other five. It could not be a dimension in space-time. Unlike the four dimensions of space and time, the fifth dimension is not an aspect of the vortex of energy. Rather, it underlies the vortex and the four dimensions associated with it.

A body would not travel in the fifth dimension by moving faster or slower. Movement in the fifth dimension would only be possible through change in the intrinsic speed of energy. We have already described this process as transubstantiation. Transubstantiation is movement in the fifth dimension. It involves change in substance, rather than change in form or position. In transubstantiation, bodies travelling in the fifth dimension appear and disappear as they leave one realm of the universe and turn up in another.

Power over the fifth dimension is the power of the gods. This power could account for miracles such as those performed by Sai Baba today and Jesus Christ two thousand years ago. The fifth dimension is the dimension of the gods. It could appropriately be called the *Deific* dimension.

But what are the gods? Where do they fit into this picture? We know that the physical universe contains life and intelligence. But ours is only a small part of a greater whole. Because there are living, intelligent beings in this small corner of the universe it would be reasonable to suppose that life and intelligence exist in the universe at large. There could be beings very much more powerful and intelligent than us, existing in the super-physical realms.

Tradition has it that there are whole hosts of super-physical beings. Ancient pagan religions all described a pantheon of gods. But not all supernatural beings were described as gods. The Greeks and Romans also recognised nature spirits: nymphs and fauns, satyrs and dryads, all under the dominion of the god Pan. In Western and Northern Europe, their equivalents were elves, fairies and pixies. Alongside these beings from other realms, were thought to exist the souls of human beings departed from this life. There is a hierarchy of life forms on Earth; it is natural that there would also be a hierarchy of supernatural beings. The term 'gods' has generally been reserved for the most powerful of these beings.

The power of the gods is the power to change the intrinsic speed of energy; it is this that confers freedom to move in the fifth dimension. A god would descend through the realms by decelerating the speed of its energy.

Accelerating its energy again, it could ascend step by step into each progressively higher heavenly realm of the universe. Such beings could sweep up and down the Deific dimension from one realm of the universe to another, like the Biblical angels ascending and descending Jacob's ladder.

Some humans also appear to have had this power. Christ, Mohammed, and Babaji, for example, each on occasion vanished out of our world and sojourned in some higher realm before returning to Earth again.

Powerful angels and demons, genii and ghouls, are reported to materialise from time to time, involving themselves in human affairs. But it would seem that not all supernatural beings have the power to travel in the fifth dimension. Just as we are confined to our plane of physical reality, so many of them appear to be limited to a single level of super-physical reality, a single realm of existence.

To the gods, we humans would be as limited as chickens in a garden. Chickens eat, drink and reproduce themselves. They are conscious and alive, but limited in intelligence. The god-like creatures responsible for the garden eat, drink and reproduce themselves. They are conscious and alive, but they are far more powerful and intelligent; they can talk, read books and compose music and do many other things which the chickens can't do. They can enter or leave the chicken enclosure at will, while the chickens stay imprisoned within it. With their bird-brained mentality, the chickens limit their world to the enclosure.

Food and drink are always made available to them by the frightening god-like creatures who steal their eggs. The stupid chickens don't understand that these superior beings have built their world and bred them as well! Nor do they realise that these beings have power of life and death over them. All they know is that from time to time one of them disappears amidst a flapping of wings and a flurry of feathers, never to return! Like chickens in the garden, we humans are imprisoned in the physical universe, stuck at the lowest level of the Deific dimension.

The physical universe is like the nursery slopes of a ski resort. Beginners, confined to these gentle slopes, are restricted to the lowest speeds. Advanced skiers, having mastered their technique, can enjoy the freedom and exhilaration of faster speeds on the steep slopes higher up the mountain. Sometimes they come whooshing down to a standstill on the nursery slopes, with a swirl of snow – terrifying the beginners out of their wits!

CHAPTER 8

The Gods Appear

It was a spring day in 1916. Three small children Lucia, aged nine, Francisco, eight, and his little sister, Jacinta, six were playing near an outcrop of rocks outside the village of Fatima in Portugal. Suddenly they were startled by an ear-splitting clap of thunder, followed by a rush of wind. The children froze, dazzled by a brilliant light gliding noiselessly towards them. Within the orb of light was a boy. As he drew close, the children flung themselves to the ground in terror. The mysterious boy spoke to them saying: "*Do not fear, I am the angel of peace!*" Thus began the apparitions of Fatima, one of the most remarkable manifestations of the supernatural in this century. It was to be the first in a whole series of related events which have continued to the present day.

These apparitions in our time echo ancient myths. The legends of Greece describe how the gods descended from the heights of Olympus to warn humanity, via oracles, of impending doom. In these events, a figure from Biblical times has appeared repeatedly to warn mankind of the dangers it faces in the present age.

The 'angel of peace' appeared to the children once more in the summer and again in the autumn. The children, meanwhile, had to suffer beatings from their parents, who thought they were inventing fantastic stories. But far more outstanding events were to follow.

It was Sunday May 13th, 1917, a year after the first apparition. Lucia, Francisco and Jacinta were tending sheep in the Cova da Ira, a large pasture belonging to Lucia's father. The flock was grazing placidly and the children were again occupied in play. Suddenly, a brilliant light appeared in a sturdy holm oak tree near the children. They tried to run away but were frozen in their tracks. Within the light stood a beautiful young woman. The light surrounding her enveloped them so they were aware of her and nothing else. She told them not to be afraid, she would not harm them. The eldest girl, Lucia, plucked up courage and asked her who she was and where she had come from. She replied that she had come from heaven. Lucia then asked her what she wanted of them. She replied that she wanted them to return to this place at the same hour on the thirteenth day of every month until October; she would then tell them who she was and what she wanted. She asked if they were willing to offer themselves in service and accept any suffering that it might cause. The children agreed. As they did so, light streamed from her hands into them. The woman then rose into the sky and disappeared.

News of the mysterious visitor quickly spread in the small village. The following month, on June 13th, fifty people accompanied the children to the holm oak tree hoping to see the woman of light for themselves. At noon, the children fell into a state of rapture as the mysterious woman appeared. She was visible only to the children, but the onlookers reported that something like a cloud rose from the tree.

These events created a considerable disturbance in Fatima, and began to attract attention from further afield in Portugal. People started to flock to Fatima in large numbers.

The children were having a difficult time with their parents who thought they might be perpetrating a dreadful hoax! As their mysterious visitor had anticipated, the children were beginning to suffer; they alone saw her and the world had to take their word for it.

On July 13th, the number of onlookers had grown to 5,000 but still she was visible only to the children. They begged her to do something that everyone could see. She promised a great sign, which would be visible to everyone, on October 13th. She also gave the children what came to be known as the three predictions of Fatima. When the children reported them, a furore erupted in Portugal which spread throughout Europe. It was not every day that simple peasant children prophesied major world events.

The first prediction claimed that the Great War, then at its height, was soon going to end; however, before it did so, a revolution would take place in Russia. Great persecutions would follow, and whole nations would be destroyed, but eventually Russia would be 'converted'. The second prediction warned of another, more terrible war to follow. It would begin in the reign of a Pope to come called Pius XI – the Second World War began 22 years later in the reign of Pius XI. A third secret prediction was entrusted to Lucia alone. She was instructed to reveal it only to the authorities of the Catholic Church – but she was promised that it would be made public in the 1960s.

On August 13th, the Mayor of Fatima anticipated huge crowds. In an attempt to avoid more controversy, he had the three children arrested. They were detained in prison for three days. At first, they were offered bribes to retract their claims. When this failed, they were threatened with continued imprisonment and even told that they were to be boiled alive in a vat of oil.

Lucia was subjected to lengthy interrogations in an attempt to extract the secret third prediction. Although terrified, the children did not retract their claims; neither did Lucia betray the secret.

Over 15,000 people had gathered outside Fatima. They were angry and disappointed at the news of the arrest. Many began to leave, assuming that nothing would happen. But at noon, there was an explosion and a flash of light. The sun grew dim and a white cloud formed over the holm oak tree. It rose into the air and slowly dissolved. As the awe-struck crowd gasped in wonder, thc whole area was bathed in coloured lights.

A month later, on September 13th, the crowd gathered at Fatima was estimated at 30,000. The children, then free again, fell into trance precisely at noon. As they did so, the sun darkened, so that stars were visible in the sky. A globe of light was seen approaching from the East, which descended onto the oak tree. At the same time, what appeared to be white flower petals drifted down from the sky, dissolving before they touched the ground.

On the eve of October 13th, the day for which the great sign had been predicted, thousands of people streamed into Fatima.

With the dawn came rain. It poured in torrents. The ground was a sea of mud. Over 50,000 people waited patiently under a host of umbrellas. Sceptics were laughing and jeering because of the appalling weather. The three children arrived just before noon. The look of joyous expectation in their faces contrasted

Figure 16. Spectators watch the sun spin at Fatima, Portugal, October 13, 1917

with the strain in their parents' – who feared for their lives if nothing happened.

When noon came, the rain ceased abruptly and the clouds parted to reveal a luminous disc in the sky. As the crowd gazed in awe, the disc began to spin.

It spun faster and faster and beams of coloured lights streamed from its rim, tinting the landscape and the upturned faces of the spectators. Twelve miles away, children in another village were delighted when their school and surrounding streets and fields were bathed in this unexpected sea of colours.

After five minutes, the disc stopped spinning – only to resume again in the opposite direction. It repeated this again, before suddenly falling from the sky.

The crowd was terrified. Many thought that it was the end of the world. But the disc then rose again to merge with the sun. The sky was now clear and spectators found that they were completely dry, with no sign of the mud and rain of minutes before.

When the children came out of rapture, they said that the lady, the Blessed Virgin Mary, had told them that in one year hence, the Great War would come to an end. The two younger children, Francisco and Jacinta, died a few years later in an epidemic of influenza. The body of Jacinta never corrupted; exhumed in 1935, it was found to be in a state of perfect preservation. The eldest child, Lucia, became a Carmelite nun and is still alive today.

Apparitions of the Virgin Mary, such as those at Fatima, are amongst the best documented examples of paranormal phenomena in this century. The Virgin Mary is supposed to have lived nearly two thousand years ago. Reports that she is appearing in the 20th century may be hard to believe, but we can begin to understand them in the light of the picture we have described.

Legend has it that, after her death, the body of the Virgin Mary was not left on Earth to decay, but that it disappeared; she is said to have been 'assumed' into heaven. It could be understood from this that her body dematerialised, in the process we have described as transubstantiation. Her body, having passed intact through the light-barrier, could have been re-animated as it entered the 'heavenly' realms of super-energy. If this is so, she could now reappear on Earth simply by reversing this process. The resurrection of Christ, her son, and his subsequent appearances on Earth, could of course be explained in precisely the same way.

Some of the other phenomena associated with these appearances can be accounted for in terms of the materialisation of super-energy. Consider, for example, the arrival of the angel. At Fatima, the angel arrived in an intensely bright light accompanied by a 'thunderclap'. One possible explanation is as follows. By tradition, an angel occupies the heavenly realms as disembodied 'spirit' – pure super-energy. To appear in our world, this super-energy would have to decelerate through the light-barrier, taking on the form of waves and vortices as it does so. It is easy to imagine in this high energy event that the body would be moving very fast as it forms. In order to decelerate to a standstill on Earth, this process would have to occur out in space. The fast-moving, newly-formed body, radiating energy as brilliant light, would then descend to Earth. It would arrive with a rush of wind and before passing through the sound-barrier it would create a sonic boom. An angel materialising in this way would be able to assume any shape it chose. Appearing, as at Fatima, to a group of children, it might take on the form of a child.

Not all encounters with supernatural beings involve their descent into our world. Many 'apparitions' are psychic in nature and not physical events. In such cases, a person's consciousness appears to be elevated, enabling him or her to become aware of the supernatural being 'at home' in its own realm. Most of the apparitions at Fatima were of this nature. However, it does seem that, on the first occasion, an angel had to enter our world to invite the involvement of the children.

This event was repeated, half a century later, to herald a further, major series of apparitions. These apparitions fulfilled the promise made to Lucia that the third, secret prediction of Fatima would be revealed in the 1960s. There has been much speculation that this prediction relates to apocalyptic warnings for the end of the 20th century. When the Virgin Mary returned in the 1960s, she openly warned of the end of the present era, in a period of intense planetary transformation.

June 18th, 1961, was a cloudless summer day in the Cantabrian mountains of North West Spain. Four girls were climbing a tree on the outskirts of San Sebastian de Garabandal, a small village in the foothills. Suddenly the still air was rent with a clap of thunder. Thinking that a thunderstorm must be approaching, the children leapt from the tree and started to run home down a rocky path called the Cuadro. Conchita, the eldest girl, happened to glance up toward a grove of pines at the top of the hill. She screamed. The others turned and froze in their tracks.

At the top of the Cuadro was a brilliant orb of light, *"brighter than the sun but not dazzling to the eyes"*. In the light was the figure of a boy, about nine or ten, dressed in a blue robe. His jet black eyes were set in a face of dark complexion. The girls were terrified. As Conchita explained, *"Though it was the face of a child it seemed to have the strength of a giant within it"*.

The transfixed girls stared at him. But the strange boy only smiled and then vanished. The girls ran home, bubbling with excitement. However, when they attempted to explain what they had seen, nobody would take them seriously.

They were, after all very young. Conchita, Loli, and Jacinta were twelve and Maria Cruz was only eleven. Their parents told them to stop telling lies and packed them off to bed.

However, on Tuesday June 20th, they were playing in the Cuadro again when suddenly they were all enveloped in light. On Wednesday the same thing happened, but this time the boy appeared again. They were completely enclosed in his orb of light and were aware only of him. Conchita asked him who he was and what he wanted. He said nothing but smiled and then vanished. This happened again on Saturday June 24th and also on Sunday the 25th.

The village was abuzz with excitement. People began to follow the girls to the Cuadro to see what was happening. They saw the girls suddenly fall heavily onto their knees, with their heads thrown back and their faces frozen but radiant with joy.

On Saturday, July 1st, the boy appeared again and spoke to them for the first time. He said that he was Michael the Archangel. The girls were very surprised at this statement; he bore no resemblance to the statue of St Michael in their village church. Michael told the girls that he would return to the grove of pines on the following day and he would be accompanied by the Virgin Mary.

News went out of Garabandal like wildfire. From early on Sunday morning, a steady stream of people made their way up the mountain track connecting Garabandal to the nearest road several kilometres away. By the afternoon, the village was thronged with so many visitors that it was practically impossible to move in the streets. At 6:00pm, as the four girls made their way up the Cuadro to the grove of pines, there were hundreds of people following them.

The children saw the angel appear with another just like him. Between the two angels was a girl aged about sixteen. She was very beautiful. Dressed in a white robe and blue mantle, she was carrying a baby.

This was the beginning of a series of more than 2,000 apparitions spread over a period of four years. From 1961 to 1965, Mary appeared to the girls almost every day and very often at night as well. The girls came to regard her as a personal friend. They confided in her. She seemed to enjoy their company and gave them advice when they had problems. Sometimes she let them hold the baby which she frequently had with her. The girls, so far from becoming aloof or sanctimonious, continued to behave as normal teenagers, chewing gum and listening to the Beatles on the radio.

There was no obvious pattern to the visitations. They occurred at any time of the day or night. Usually, Mary appeared to the girls together but sometimes she came to them individually. They always knew she was about to appear from an inner feeling which they described as a 'calling'.

During the four years, doctors and scientists from many different countries studied the girls. They were impressed by their sheer normality.

They found no sign of hysteria, psychosis or neurosis; nor were the girls particularly pious. In rapture, the girls were impervious to the prick of a needle or the flame of a cigarette lighter. They also became so heavy that the strongest men in the village found it difficult to lift them. Yet, in this state, they would frequently be seen to levitate. Sometimes they moved backwards at running pace. They could move over rough ground on their knees faster than people could follow them on foot and then stop quite instantaneously. Occasionally, whilst in rapture, the girls spoke in foreign languages, or recited prayers in Greek

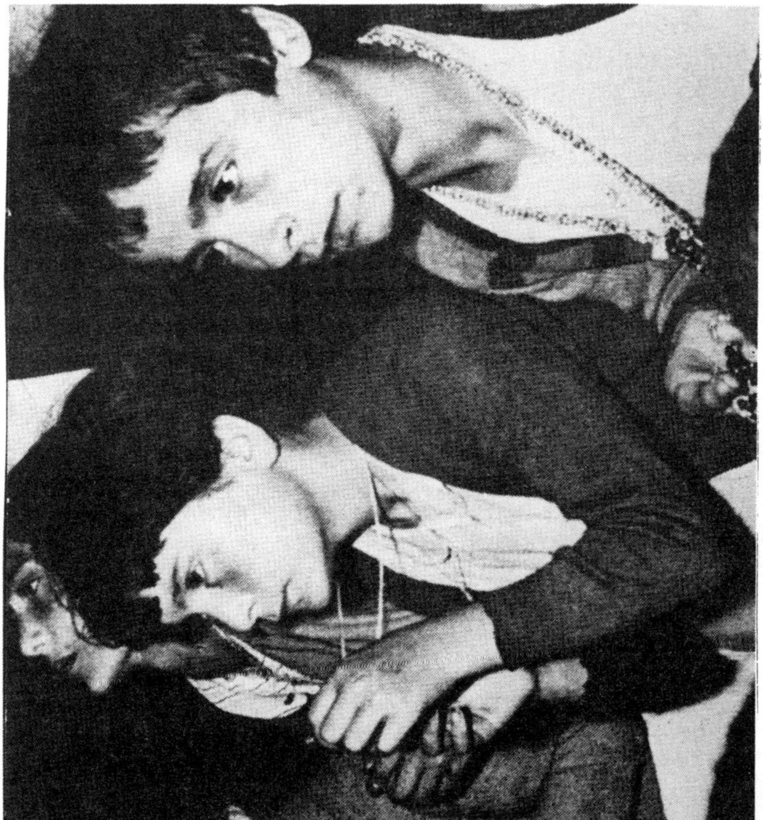

Figure 17. The girls in trance during visions of the Virgin Mary at Garabandal, Spain, 1961

or Latin. Yet normally these peasant children spoke only Spanish.

The Virgin told the girls that she had come to warn humanity. She spoke to them of impending disaster; a cataclysm would befall the world, unless mankind turned to peace. It would be preceded by a schism in the Catholic church, in which "*Cardinal would oppose cardinal and bishop would oppose bishop*". One June evening in 1962, the girls were given a vision of the disaster. They came out of trance in a state of shock and terror. In their vision, they had seen the world engulfed by fire.

The Virgin of Garabandal made two further predictions. The first concerned a supernatural event in which everything in the world would emit light for a short period of time. This 'event of light' would cause no harm but would serve as a portent of imminent disaster. It would, she said, awaken the conscience of humanity.

The second prediction foretold a 'miracle' in Garabandal, to take place within a year of the event of light. Conchita alone has been entrusted with the date of this event, which she has been asked to release eight days in advance. Conchita has said that the miracle will be seen by anyone in Garabandal or in the hills around it. Conchita has also been told that a supernatural sign will be left as a permanent reminder in the grove of pines. It will be seen, photographed and televised, but will not be tangible or measurable in any other way.

The predictions of Garabandal have been greeted with scepticism by many people.

However, they closely resemble other prophecies for the closing decade of the 20th century. Seers including Nostradamus, Edgar Cayce, Jean Dixon, Paul Solomon and many others have forecast an unprecedented wave of calamities for this period. Their visions include war, earthquakes and volcanoes, and the flooding of major cities by the rising of the oceans. Famine, new plagues, and a cataclysm caused by a comet are also part of this apocalyptic scenario. There are those who see these predicted patterns emerging in the greenhouse effect, AIDS, and the increasing frequency of severe earthquakes. However the future is not immutable. Furthermore, in all these prophecies, it has been intimated that the disasters can be diminished in scale, or even averted, by change in the consciousness of humanity. It may be that prophets serve to warn us of dangers on the road we are taking, so that we have the opportunity to change direction and so avert disaster. Prophets in the past have often been proved wrong.

In Garabandal, as at Fatima, the Virgin appeared only to a small group of children and not to bystanders. The next sequence of apparitions was entirely different. In them, the Virgin appeared, not to a small number of selected individuals, but to tens of thousands of people. These dramatic apparitions occurred in Egypt in 1968. They are unprecedented in the annals of the paranormal. The extraordinary events which took place were photographed and even televised, appearing on news broadcasts around the world.

On the night of April 2nd, 1968, two mechanics were working at a garage in Zeitoun, a northern suburb of Cairo. Legend has it that Zeitoun is the site of the village which harboured Joseph, Mary and Jesus when, as described in the New Testament, they fled the wrath of Herod.

The two mechanics noticed something strange on the roof of an Orthodox Coptic church on the opposite side of the road. It seemed to them that a nun, in a white habit, was standing on the central dome of the church, holding onto the stone cross on top of it. Thinking that she must be attempting suicide, one mechanic telephoned the fire brigade to bring her down; the other ran off for the priest to persuade her not to jump.

On his arrival, the priest quickly realised that this was not a nun attempting suicide, but something quite different. The police then arrived and a crowd began to gather. The woman in a brilliant white robe was now bathed in so much light that it lit up the night sky.

Night after night, the apparition was repeated. People began to flock to Zeitoun, first by the hundreds then in thousands. Over a period of time, hundreds of thousands of people came to witness the phenomena, most of them Muslims or Coptic Christians.

Spectators agreed that the form was that of a woman, but usually the light radiating from her was too bright to discern her features clearly. Her appearances were frequently heralded by mysterious lights and glowing clouds.

Figure 18. An apparition of the Virgin Mary on the roof of the church at Zeitoun, Egypt, 1968

Often, large, luminous figures with wings glided in suddenly from the East. Up to a dozen of these objects were sometimes seen flying in the formation of a cross or triangle. They would then vanish as abruptly as lights being switched off. Very often, a luminous bird was seen hovering above the head of the woman.

One night, a strange mist-like substance poured out from beneath one of the small domes of the church. Emitting light, it crept up all over the roof until the entire structure and the air surrounding it appeared to be ablaze.

On another occasion, vast clouds of glowing, red incense billowed up from the great central dome of the church. Clouds of this luminous incense appeared from nowhere and drifted down amongst the vast throng of people gathered around the church. At times the woman would appear with a clearly discernible baby in one hand and an olive branch in the other. Occasionally she was joined by a boy. Sometimes the form of a man appeared as well. Like the woman, these forms were radiant with bluish-white light and difficult to discern. These paranormal events often lasted for hours. On June 8th, 1968, for instance, they began at 9:00pm and continued until 4:30am.

There were many reports of miraculous healing. Over the three years of the apparitions, thousands of people were spontaneously healed of diseases including cancer, arthritis, blindness, paralysis and gangrene. Even those who were not anticipating any alleviation of their infirmity were cured. Many of these cases of instant healing were documented by the professor of medicine at Ain Shams University, who headed a commission of seven doctors that studied the cures. Other scientists from the Egyptian universities were instructed by their government to investigate the phenomenon. They concluded that the apparitions were genuine and paranormal in origin.

After these findings, the government arranged for the demolition of buildings around the church to make space for the increasingly large gatherings of visitors, who were beginning to come in from all over the world. Before long, however, some enterprising bureaucrats decided to treat the apparitions as a tourist attraction. They cordoned off the area around the church and started to charge people for admission. When this happened, the apparitions first became dim and indistinct and then eventually ceased altogether.

The apparitions at Zeitoun are exceptionally rich in supernatural phenomena. The common strand could be seen as the transubstantiation of super-energy into energy. This 'condensation' through the light-barrier could explain not only the figures that appeared but also the mysterious lights, luminous mists and glowing clouds of incense. These effects resemble the manifestations of *ectoplasm* common in the seances of the nineteenth century.

The most distinctive feature of these apparitions is of course that the Virgin Mary appeared to enter our world. At Fatima and Garabandal, she was only seen by 'visionaries' in trance. By contrast, at Zeitoun she was visible to everyone who happened to be there. As we have already seen, this phenomenon can also be accounted for in terms of transubstantiation. The Virgin could appear on Earth as the energy within every vortex of her 'assumed' body decelerates through the light-barrier. By this means, she could appear instantly and silently wherever and whenever she chose.

The Virgin returned to Earth on her own, silently and unexpectedly, almost twenty years to the day after the start of the Garabandal events. This, the most recent appearance of the Virgin Mary, occurred in the outlying district of Medjugorje, in Yugoslavia. To date, upwards of 15 million people have trekked from all over the world as pilgrims to this remote Yugoslavian village. Lasting for the best part of a decade, these daily apparitions form the longest series on record.

The Medjugorje apparitions have not been without accompanying paranormal phenomena. There have been 150 documented healings. Strong lights often appear around a concrete cross on top of a nearby hill, and strange lights in the sky at night sometimes taking the form of the word "Mir" meaning peace.

Many pilgrims claim to have seen the sun dance, others report that their rosaries have been miraculously turned into gold.

As at Fatima and Garabandal, Mary appeared at Medjugorje principally to a small group of young people. She is said to have spoken to them of heaven and hell and given them visions of these states. However, she has assured them that "*God never sends anyone to hell*"; God is not a judge who condemns sinners to hell, rather people choose hell for themselves. Her main message has been a call for peace. Prophecy has again featured. She has given the visionaries ten predictions of major world events, to be made public shortly before each event occurs. They will serve to validate the apparitions and help people to believe in the supernatural. Furthermore a supernatural sign will emerge on the hill where she first appeared.

Marian apparitions in the 20th century are amongst the most astonishingly rich displays of the supernatural on record. As well as those we have described, there have been others in France, Lebanon, the Ukraine and Ireland.

In addition to this, the 20th century has seen the reappearance of supernatural beings from the pagan tradition, as we shall see in the next chapter.

CHAPTER 9

The return of Pan

In pagan religions, there were held to be many gods with different roles. Some were thought to look down and judge us from on high, occasionally descending in a spectacular way to intervene in human affairs. Others were said to toil behind the scenes, involving themselves in our world subtly and invisibly.

Many pagan traditions held that the natural order was the handiwork of the gods. The world of nature was said to be under the dominion of a major deity known as Pan. He was thought to preside over a host of nature spirits held to be responsible for the fine detail.

Legend has it that in antiquity men and women communed with these gods and nature spirits quite frequently. Today people who claim to see gnomes, elves and fairies are generally ridiculed. Nonetheless there are people who claim not only to have seen them, but also to have cooperated with them over many years. One such group is based in Scotland. Their dramatic and prolonged encounters with nature spirits have made them world-famous. These events began quite suddenly and unexpectedly in the early 1960s.

Peter Caddy was the perfect English gentleman, a one-time Squadron Leader in the R.A.F. In 1960, he was comfortably installed as manager of a luxury hotel overlooking the Moray Firth in Scotland. Nearby in the Bay of Findhorn was a windswept caravan park. More than once, as he drove by it, the thought crossed his mind, "Fancy living in a place like that, cheek by jowl in those tiny caravans".

It was a miserable, bitterly cold day in November 1962. Amidst icy blasts and flurries of snow, Peter Caddy found himself moving onto the caravan park.

With his wife Eileen, their three small boys, and a colleague from the hotel, Dorothy Maclean, he was manoeuvring a thirty foot caravan onto the desolate site. He and his family had been struck a sudden and unexpected double blow, homelessness and unemployment.

The weeks of unemployment turned into months and the months into years.

Peter applied for job after job but to no avail. He had good references and experience, but something always seemed to block him. He never gave up trying nor lost faith. He firmly believed that his fate was in the hands of God.

Officers from the local Unemployment Benefit Office appeared to share this sentiment. An inspector who interviewed Peter expressed grave misgivings. Why had Peter Caddy, with his blue-chip background, been relying on state benefit for so long? Peter explained that he had complete faith in God and had never ceased in his efforts to find work but that something seemed to block his way.

The officer then asked, "Would you say that God is preventing you from getting a job?".

Peter was taken aback at this unexpected question. He found himself replying, "Why yes, indeed".

"Well then", said the officer, "presumably if we cut off your benefit, God will provide for you." Peter had to reply that he thought that was true and so they cut off his unemployment benefit forthwith.

In his first spring at the caravan park, Peter had decided to try his luck at growing a few vegetables to occupy his time and help feed his impoverished family. He was faced with an impossible task. He pored over gardening books but they were written for fertile gardens in the mild English climate. There was little advice on how to grow vegetables on a sand-dune in the cold, wet climate of Scotland. The land around his caravan was just a tangle of couch grass in sand, gravel and rocks, constantly exposed to salt-laden winds howling in off the North Sea. The very idea of establishing a vegetable plot there was bizarre.

Whilst Peter battled with the couch grass in his seemingly hopeless task of establishing a garden, Eileen was receiving 'guidance' through meditation.

She was told that their every need would be met. Her husband should go on applying for jobs, but the time was not yet right.

Figure 19. Peter and Eileen Caddy

To Peter, it seemed that the most important thing was to persevere with the garden. He fenced off a good sized plot of ground to protect it from wind and rabbits. With help from Eileen, Dorothy and the boys, he collected horse dung from neighbouring fields. By salvaging straw, seaweed and vegetable waste for compost, he built up a meagre layer of humus in the sand and began planting seeds.

Both Eileen and Dorothy were now receiving guidance about the garden.

Gradually it dawned on them that they were to take part in a pioneering experiment. In their work in the garden, they were going to be assisted by nature spirits. The supernatural beings behind nature were joining forces with them. With the help of the 'little people' – gnomes, elves and fairies – the Caddys would create something of importance to the world.

As they began to follow the instructions they were receiving, the dunes were transformed. From the Findhorn sands, as barren as a desert, there sprang forth flowers and lush green vegetables unprecedented for their yield and vigour. Every plant in the garden flourished. Within a few months, flowers blossomed everywhere. Visitors left shaking their heads in disbelief; how could there be so much greenness and vitality when everything around was dry and dead? Later, vegetables grew to an enormous size. Findhorn became famous for giant cabbages weighing as much as forty pounds! Not only was there sufficient to feed the Caddys but the garden provided a surplus to sell in the neighbourhood.

Over the next few years, the garden's reputation grew and people came from far and wide to view it. Horticultural experts were completely dumbfounded. Professor R. Lindsay Robb, at one time an agricultural consultant to the United Nations, reported of the garden,

> The vigour, health and bloom of the plants in this garden at midwinter on land which is almost barren powdery sand cannot be explained by the moderate dressings of compost nor indeed by the application of any known cultural methods of organic husbandry. There are other factors and they are vital ones.

Early in the garden's development, Dorothy Maclean had found herself in communication with supernatural beings called *devas* – the spirits of entire plant species. Dorothy provided a direct link between the devas and the Caddy family, guiding them in the day to day work of planting, tending and harvesting. The devas gave such advice as where to place particular vegetable types for best results, and how far apart to plant them.

In *The Findhorn Garden*, Dorothy describes the *devas* as part of a whole hierarchy of spiritual beings involved in the natural world, "from the earthiest gnome to the highest archangel". She explains that the *devas* might be considered as 'architects', supervising the work of building up mineral, vegetable and animal forms.

> The devas hold the archetypal pattern and plan for all forms around us, and they direct the energy needed for materialising them . . . While the devas might be considered the 'architects' of plant forms. the nature spirits or elementals, such as gnomes and fairies, may be seen as the 'craftsmen', using the blueprint and energy channelled to them by the devas . . .

According to Dorothy, these supernatural beings deal directly with energy. They experience the garden, not as material, but

Figure 20. Dorothy Maclean

as forms of energy behind the physical structures that we see. She quotes them as saying,

> We do not see things as you do, in their solid, outer materialisations, but rather in their inner life-giving state. We deal with what is behind what you see or sense, but these are interconnected, like different octaves of the same melody.

To them, the garden was not an assembly of various forms and colours,

> . . . but rather moving lines of energy . . . within this field of energy, each plant was an individual whirlpool of activity.

A further invaluable link between this hierarchy of spirits and man emerged through a Scotsman, R. Ogilvie Crombie, who became closely associated with Findhorn. Crombie – affectionately known as 'Roc' – found himself communicating directly with individual nature spirits. Roc was able to relay specific messages back to the Caddys working in the garden. For example, when Peter Caddy was in the process of chopping down some gorse bushes, it was Roc who informed him that he was disturbing the gnomes!

Roc was at first reluctant to speak publicly about his extraordinary experiences. Like most people, he was inclined to dismiss belief in gnomes, elves and fairies as superstition. But over time he became convinced of the reality of these beings and talked quite openly about them. The account which follows is taken from his description of a series of quite spectacular experiences. It is given here at length because it points to the possibility that not only the nature spirits but also the gods of ancient mythology are more than mere figments of imagination.

One afternoon in March 1966, Roc was walking in the Royal Botanic Gardens of Edinburgh. He sat down under a spreading beech tree. Suddenly he noticed a small figure dancing in front of him only twenty or so yards away. It was about three feet tall. To his complete amazement, Roc realised that it was a faun as described in mythology. It was half human, half animal. It had a pointed chin and ears and two little horns on its forehead. Its shaggy legs ended in cloven hooves and its skin was honey-coloured. The creature seemed quite real and solid – Roc had

Figure 21. R. Ogilvie Crombie – 'Roc'

wondered at first if it was a schoolboy dressed up for a play. He watched in astonishment, hardly able to believe his eyes.

The faun danced over to Roc and sat down in front of him. Roc lent forward and said, "Hello"!

The faun sprang to its feet in amazement. "Can you see me?", it asked.

"Yes", replied Roc.

The faun responded, "I don't believe it. Humans can't see us". It asked Roc to describe its appearance, which he did. The faun then danced a jig and asked him what it was doing. Roc described its antics, at which the faun replied, "You must be seeing me!".

The faun, whose name was Kurmos, then sat down next to Roc and asked, "Why are human beings so stupid?" He said that many of the nature spirits had lost interest in the human race, since they have been made to feel neither believed in nor wanted. "If you think you can get along without us, just try!"

Kurmos explained that he lived in the Gardens and that his work was to help the growth of the trees. Roc invited him back to his flat. The faun had never been inside a human house before and accepted the invitation with delight. As Roc walked through the streets of Edinburgh, with Kurmos at his side, he wondered how the busy shoppers would react if they could see what he was seeing.

In Roc's flat, Kurmos was fascinated by the rows of books in the bookshelves. When Roc explained what they were for, Kurmos was amazed. "Why", he exclaimed, "surely you can get all the knowledge you want by simply wanting it!" When Kurmos left the flat, he ran lightly down the stairs but vanished before reaching the front door.

The next time Roc visited the Botanical Gardens he called the faun's name and Kurmos appeared. These unusual meetings were a source of profound satisfaction to Roc. They turned out to be the prelude to even more astounding events.

Late one night in April, Roc was walking down Princes Street in Edinburgh.

Suddenly he stepped into what he could only describe as an extraordinary atmosphere. It was denser than air and made him feel warm and tingling like a mixture of pins and needles and electric shock. At the same time his awareness was heightened and he had a great feeling of expectation.

Then he realised that he wasn't alone. A faun, taller than he, was walking beside him. It radiated tremendous power. They walked on in silence for a few moments. Suddenly it turned to Roc and whispered, "Well, aren't you afraid of me?"

"No", replied Roc.

"Why not? All human beings are afraid of me!", exclaimed the extraordinary figure.

"I feel no evil in your presence", declared Roc. "I see no reason why you should want to harm me. I do not feel afraid".

"Do you know who I am?", it asked.

At that moment Roc suddenly realised who the figure was. "You are the great god Pan!"

"Then you ought to be afraid", Pan replied, "Your word 'panic' comes from the fear my presence causes".

"Not always", said Roc, quietly and calmly, "I am not afraid".

"Can you give me a reason?", demanded Pan.

"It may be because of my feeling of affinity with your subjects, the earth spirits and woodland creatures", explained Roc.

"Do you believe in my subjects?"

"Yes!"

"Do you love my subjects?"

"Yes, I do."

"In that case, do you love me?"

"Why not?"

"Do you love me?"

"Yes!"

Pan looked at Roc with a strange smile and a deep glint in his mysterious brown eyes. "You know, of course, I'm the devil!", he whispered. "You have just said you love the devil!"

"No, you are not the devil", retorted Roc. "You are the god of the woodlands and countryside. There is no evil in you. You are Pan."

"Did the early Christian Church not take me as a model for the devil", exclaimed Pan. "Look at my cloven hooves, my shaggy legs and the horns on my forehead!"

"Ah! but the Church turned all pagan gods and spirits into devils, fiends and imps", replied Roc.

"Was the Church wrong then?", enquired Pan.

"The Church acted with the best intentions", explained Roc,

"but it was wrong. The ancient gods are not necessarily devils."

Pan was now walking very close to Roc. "You don't mind me walking beside you?", he asked. "You really feel no repulsion or fear?"

"None."

"Excellent!" exclaimed Pan.

Roc then asked Pan if he had his pipes. Pan smiled at the request and replied, "I do have them you know." And there they were, between his hands.

Pan began to play a curious melody. Roc realised he had heard it in the woods before, but it had been so elusive he had never been able to remember it afterwards. By then they had reached Roc's home. As Roc stepped up to the front door, Pan disappeared.

In May, Roc and Peter Caddy went on a visit to the small island of Iona off the coast of Scotland. They were standing in a ring of stones, the site of a hermit's cell. This place was said to be where St Columba went on retreat.

Suddenly Roc was aware of a large figure lying on the ground in front of them. It appeared to be a monk in a brown habit with a hood over the head.

The figure rose silently from the ground and pulled back the hood. It was Pan.

He smiled and declared:

> I am the servant of Almighty God. I and all my subjects are willing to come to the aid of mankind, in spite of the way he has treated us and abused nature. We will help if he affirms belief in us and asks for our help.

In September, Roc met Pan again. Roc was at a weekend conducted by Sir George Trevelyan at Attingham Park, an adult education and conference centre housed in a stately home in Shropshire. What occurred then is best described in his own words:

> Before leaving on Monday morning, I was prompted to go to an area known as The Mile Walk on Attingham's extensive and beautiful grounds. I followed the path until I came to the Rhododendron Walk which is considered by some to be a place of great spiritual power.

At its entrance is a huge cedar tree with a bench beneath it. I sat there for some time, enjoying the beauty of the place, then rose and entered the Walk. As I did so, I felt a great build-up of power and a vast increase in awareness. Colours and forms became more significant. I was aware of every single leaf on the bushes and trees, of every blade of grass on the path standing out with startling clarity. It was as if physical reality had become much more real than it normally is, and the three dimensional effect we are used to had become even more solid. This kind of experience is nearly impossible to describe in words. I had the impression of complete reality, and all that lies within and beyond it felt immediately imminent. There was an acute feeling of being one with nature in a complete way, as well as being one with the divine, which produced great exultation, and a deep sense of awe and wonder.

I became aware of Pan walking by my side and of a strong bond between us. He stepped behind me and then walked into me so that we became one, and I saw the surroundings through his eyes. At the same time, part of me – the recording, observing part – stood aside. The experience was not a form of possession but of identification, a kind of integration.

The moment he stepped into me the woods became alive with myriad beings – elementals, nymphs, dryads, fauns, elves, gnomes, fairies and so on, far too numerous to catalogue. They varied in size from tiny little beings a fraction of an inch in height – like the ones I saw swarming about on a clump of toadstools – to beautiful elfin creatures, three or four inches tall. Some of them danced around me in a ring; all were welcoming and full of rejoicing. The nature spirits love and delight in the work they do and express this in movement.

I felt as if I were outside time and space. Everything was happening in the now. It is impossible to give more than a faint impression of the actuality of this experience, but I would stress the exultation and the feeling of joy and delight. Yet there was an underlying peace, contentment and a sense of spiritual presence.

The events and concepts associated with the Findhorn Garden may be regarded as far-fetched by many people. These unusual experiences of the supernatural are easy to reject out of hand or dismiss as absurd. Sceptics may be inclined to treat these accounts as wishful thinking; it is easy to say that these experiences occurred only in the mind. Pan and the nature spirits are often taken not to be real, but to be mere hallucinations or figments of the imagination.

Many people regard angels, fairies and such-like as purely psychic phenomena, implying that they exist only in the minds of those who claim to see them. By contrast, we are suggesting that these supernatural entities are not mere 'psychic' fantasy, but are real forms of energy which are being perceived with faculties that most of us would seem to have lost. Blind to these realities, we treat them with incredulity.

Roc was trained as a scientist and admits that the mind plays a major part in his 'communications'. He is not seeing with his eyes or hearing with his ears. Beings such as Kurmos, 'living' in the gardens, are inhabitants of another plane of existence. The words he hears in his head, Roc says, probably arise as thoughts projected into his mind which are then translated by his consciousness.

The mind is obviously involved in these experiences. But rather than pure invention, its role could be to give form to otherwise amorphous energy fields. It is not that these beings are purely mythical, but that we cloak them in familiar mythological garb, perhaps dredged up from the collective unconscious.

Dorothy Maclean's account of the nature spirits supports this idea. According to her, these beings have no particular form, rather their form changes as they travel from realm to realm. In contact with humans, they become become visible in a form *intelligible* to us:

> Their forms reflect their functions. For instance a dwarf is usually depicted with a pickaxe, denoting our human interpretation of his work with the mineral kingdom. Angels, on the other hand, are portrayed with wings, and often as bearing something . . .

In other words, these beings may appear to have a particular form, but they are not in truth restricted to one form or place. Pan, for example, is a 'universal energy'.

Most of us nowadays have no awareness of nature spirits or

other supernatural beings at all. We don't have the appropriate 'sensitivity' to see them; Kurmos, the faun, was very surprised to be seen by Roc; he was accustomed to being invisible.

It would appear though that supernatural beings are keenly aware of us. Kurmos, Pan, and the gnomes in the Findhorn garden were all very familiar with humans.

Supernatural beings would be aware of our world because it falls within their overall domain; our world is part of the greater supernatural environment. It is as if these nature spirits are just outside our space-time, observing us from beyond the light-barrier. The light-barrier could be likened to a one-way mirror. To most of us, it is completely opaque; we cannot 'see' through it into other worlds. Supernatural beings, however, would appear to be able to look through it at us.

We are aware of the physical world through our senses, which detect forms of energy in our environment, translate them into nerve signals, and communicate this information as vibrations to the brain. In the higher realms, intelligent beings must be able to detect super-energy directly, in order to perceive their world. They may also be able to 'tune into' the vibrations of the slower energy in our physical domain. In this way they could be aware of light and matter.

As humans, we have only a limited perception of energy. Our sense of sight, for instance, is limited to the visible spectrum; if we saw with x-rays, we would have a totally different picture of the world. Even in the physical world, there is a great deal going on to which we are blind.

Beings in the higher realms may well be limited in similar ways. They would not all be aware of everything in our realm in precisely the same way or to the same extent. Some occupants of higher realms may 'see' our world much as we do. Others, however, operating on a different frequency band, might be more aware of the energy patterns, invisible to us, which lie behind the physical forms in our world. Yet others may be completely unaware of us.

The Findhorn experience confirms this picture. Dorothy MacLean's account strongly suggests that nature spirits operate on energies behind the physical forms in our world, rather than on matter itself; they are more aware of the energies behind the plants than they are of the plants themselves.

The idea that there really are nature spirits at work behind the scenes has suggested to some people the possibility of a new approach to the problems of pollution and atmospheric warming. Tradition has it that each element is served by diverse 'elementals' specific to it: *sylphs* for the air, *undines* for water; *gnomes* for earth; and *salamanders* for fire. Some people believe that by seeking the cooperation of these beings, we could address many of our ecological problems. This form of cooperation, was after all, what the Findhorn experiment was all about. These beings, however, will not act alone to resolve the problems we have created. The initiative must come from man.

It would be misleading to leave this chapter without acknowledging the role of Findhorn today. From these beginnings, Findhorn has grown into a broadly based spiritual community, of around 200 members. While the garden still plays a part, the community has extended its vision of cooperation to other areas of activity, and is highly regarded around the world as one of the focal points of 'new age' awareness.

Some people say that the supernatural awareness reputedly enjoyed by many people in the past will one day return. If so, the extraordinary events surrounding the early days of Findhorn could turn out to be at the vanguard of human experience. Those who claim to see fairies, elves and gnomes at work in nature may be perceiving a reality that many people will come to experience for themselves in the future.

The puzzling phenomenon of crop circles, for example, may be pointing to this hidden reality. Crop circles, which seem to be proliferating, could be another way that nature spirits are now interacting with man. Certainly, the greater man's interest, the more abundant and complex these patterns appear to become. It could be that in crop circles we are witnessing nature spirits sporting with man. For example, when two leading investigators said to each other that they had now 'grasped the phenomenon by its tail', they were rewarded a few days later by the appearance of a vast circle with a magnificent tail! Then, when a crop watch was mounted, no circles appeared, but as the watchers dispersed, they found that a circle had mysteriously appeared in a field behind them. This playful behaviour is said to be typical of some nature spirits, who, like young children, thrive on attention and delight in pranks.

We have mostly been brought up in an atmosphere of fear surrounding the supernatural. Supernatural beings undoubtedly have power, but they are not all necessarily malevolent. We could look on them much as we look on people on Earth. They are simply beings without physical bodies, and they differ as much from each other as we do. Some may be mischievous, on occasion, but it would be ridiculous to fear fauns, gnomes, and fairies. In the past, many supernatural beings were judged to be evil; in reality, it may be that most of the evil has its origin in the shadows of the human mind, from where it is projected out onto the higher realms.

But is the earth really a garden, in which nature spirits labour? If there really are supernatural beings at work behind nature, how do they operate? If they have an important part to play in life on earth, what sense can we make of them in the light of modern biology? We shall see in the next chapter.

CHAPTER 10

The Secret of Life

In times gone by, life was seen as something sacred, wrought by the hand of God. Today, most people see no role for the divine in nature; they look instead to science to explain the mystery of life. Universities and biological research laboratories have no place for Pan. The notion that nature spirits are responsible for the order of life on Earth would strike most biologists as totally absurd. Even the idea of God as creator has been made redundant.

Contemporary biology has reduced life to the interactions of atoms and molecules, to pure biochemistry. Biologists admit that there are still major problems to be solved. But generally they believe that everything about life will be explained, eventually, in terms of existing biological principles. Some even consider that biology is in sight of completing this task.

The scientific account of life centres on the theory of evolution proposed by Charles Darwin (1809-1882). Darwin's theory appears to make the idea of a divine creator and designer completely redundant. It explains the origin and diversity of life without recourse to anything supernatural whatsoever.

Darwin's idea was that, aeons ago, life first appeared on Earth quite spontaneously; these first flickers of life came about as a result of the random association of chemical substances. Darwin envisaged the crucible of life in which these reactions first occurred as "some warm little pond"; nowadays scientists talk of a 'primordial soup' in the early seas. Here, chemicals such as nitrogen, carbon, oxygen and hydrogen are believed to have reacted together to form the basic building blocks of life. These gradually merged, with the passage of time, to form the first primitive cells – which in turn came together to give rise to multicellular organisms. Then, over the course of millions of years, successive generations of organisms underwent a series of minute changes. Through a process of 'natural selection', those offspring with characteristics that benefited them in their struggle for survival flourished to reproduce their kind; those with disadvantageous inherited characteristics perished. In this ruthless test of nature, only beneficial variations survived. Over millions upon millions of years, this gradual process is supposed to have selected out all the diverse species of plant and animal life present on the planet today.

In Charles Darwin's own words:

> Natural selection is daily and hourly scrutinising throughout the world the slightest variations, rejecting those that are bad, preserving and adding up all that are good, silently and insensibly working.

Darwin's ideas have been a great source of inspiration to free-thinkers in both the 19th and 20th centuries. The theory of evolution was a major insight. In botany and zoology there is now an enormous weight of evidence to support it. Few scientists doubt that a process of evolution occurs on Earth.

There are innumerable examples of the process of evolution and natural selection at work. The development of worms serves as a good example. The first multicellular animals had unbroken tissue between their outer skin surface and the inner lining of their guts. The corals and jellyfish are an example of these primitive two-layer types of animal. Many of us have met their humble little representative *hydra* in biology laboratories at school or college.

These organisms were very successful when rooted on one spot. Like the sea anemone, they sat with their tentacles wafting in the water ready to catch minute particles of food which drifted their way. But problems arose when these simple two-layer animals attempted to move.

The earliest types of worm were based on the two-layer model. The locomotion of worms is based upon waves of contraction passing down their body. Now it is precisely this process, known as peristalsis, which is employed by the gut in swallowing food.

These early worms had a real problem. With no separation between their skin and their gut, their movement toward food would cause food already swallowed to be expelled. Then, having found some food, the action of swallowing would move them away from it, just when they were settling down to a meal. They had a design fault which made 'life on the open range' very difficult: they had to move in order to eat, but they couldn't eat without moving.

The harsh process of natural selection might have destined these unfortunate creatures to extinction. However, they adapted and outwitted their executioner; they found a niche in which they could eat without having to move: they became parasites. The flatworms that cause the terrible disease bilharzia, afflicting millions of people in Africa and Asia, and the liver flukes that plague sheep and cattle – not to mention the gruesome tapeworms – are their modern descendants.

However, quite suddenly, a new type of worm appeared with a split between its gut and its skin. This creature could move without upsetting its digestion and eat without leaving the table between each mouthful. The earthworm is an example of this improved, mark II model worm. All subsequent locomoting animals, ourselves included, have this 'design modification' built in. We all have a cavity in a third layer of tissues between the gut and the skin.

Darwin attributed this type of development to chance variations.

According to his theory, amongst millions of early worms struggling to eat without moving and move without defecating, a change must have occurred. A fluke variation must have arisen that led to a cavity arising between the skin and gut in a worm. This creature, able to eat without moving, would have had an advantage over his fellows. He would then have passed on this advantageous characteristic to future generations of worms.

In this century, the discovery of DNA has provided an understanding of inheritance mechanisms that Darwin lacked. The DNA molecule has been identified as the genetic material through which characteristics are transmitted from generation to generation. The fundamental Darwinian concept of random variations has been re-expressed in terms of random changes in DNA.

So a school of neo-Darwinism has grown up with greater refinement than Darwin's original theory. Yet the original Darwinian view that evolution is based fundamentally upon chance remains unchanged.

Despite all this, there is still considerable resistance to evolutionary theory. Many people find it impossible to believe that random changes in the chemical structure of DNA are sufficient to explain evolution. They cannot accept that the amazing diversity of life is based purely upon blind chance with no intelligence or design behind it.

One argument against Darwinian evolution centres on the infrequency of beneficial variations. Contemporary biologists are convinced that all changes in DNA are mistakes in its copying. Yet the structure of DNA is remarkably stable; in fact, scientists are amazed at how rarely mistakes occur in its repeated copying. Moreover, when mistakes do occur, they are very rarely advantageous. How likely is it that sufficient beneficial variations could arise purely by chance? According to this argument, even the millions of years in the history of this planet do not allow sufficient time for this haphazard process to have produced the amazing variety and complexity of life on Earth.

Another area of doubt concerns the role of DNA. It is not clear that differences in DNA alone can account for major differences in species. For instance, there is very little difference between the DNA of humans and that of chimpanzees; closely related species of mice differ more in their DNA than do humans and chimpanzees. Furthermore, only about 1% of DNA appears to be used genetically. To some people it seems that DNA represents an overall 'pool of possibility'. Perhaps something *switches on* a different set of genes in a chimpanzee to a human; maybe some external factor selects particular genetic patterns from the pool, while others lie fallow and unexplored.

One scientist to have argued vociferously against Darwin's theory of evolution is the astronomer Sir Fred Hoyle. In his book *The Intelligent Universe*, he reasons that evolution must be driven by intelligence. He even speculates on 'gods' – invisible, intelligent forces acting as 'managers' of evolution. Hoyle considers it a vast unlikelihood that life could have evolved from non-living matter without the intervention of intelligence.

As he says,

> . . . it is apparent that the origin of life is overwhelmingly a matter of arrangement, of ordering quite common atoms into very special structures and sequences. Whereas we learn in physics that non-living processes tend to destroy order,

> intelligent control is particularly effective at producing order out of chaos. You might even say that intelligence shows itself most effectively in arranging things, exactly what the origin of life requires.

Neo-Darwinists vehemently deny that intelligence or any other external factor is involved in the origin and evolution of life. In his celebrated book *The Blind Watchmaker*, the Oxford biologist Richard Dawkins is emphatic on this point. Complex organisation does exist in nature, he says – but there is no overall sense of direction and certainly no designer. The process of natural selection which drives evolution is completely blind. Dawkins accepts that the origin and evolution of life does require a whole sequence of highly improbable events. But in his view, over millions upon millions of years, "near miracles" could have occurred. Evolution is cumulative. Each tiny step would build on all the others. The process could go a long way on a few 'lucky breaks'.

Because it is conceivable that evolution could have happened in this way, biologists such as Dawkins argue that extraneous factors are not necessary. They believe that chance alone is responsible for the variations that are tested by natural selection – and that the variations themselves are merely mistakes in the copying of DNA, perhaps caused by cosmic rays. They take it that the fantastic diversity of life on Earth is nothing but the culmination of a series of such chance mistakes and they regard any other explanation as superfluous.

This concept is central to modern biology. As the Nobel prize-winner Jacques Monod says:

> Chance alone is at the source of every innovation, of all creation . . . Pure chance, absolutely free but blind, at the very root of the stupendous edifice of evolution: this central concept of modern biology is no longer one among other conceivable hypotheses. It is today the sole conceivable hypothesis . . .

But is this account really the 'sole conceivable hypothesis'? The events of evolution took place hundreds of millions of years ago and nearly all the evidence has disappeared. As the biologist Rupert Sheldrake acknowledges:

> Very little is known or can ever be known about the details

> of evolution in the past. Nor is evolution readily observable in the present . . . With such scanty direct evidence, and with so little possibility of experimental test, any interpretation of the mechanism of evolution is bound to be speculative.

Does the whole edifice of evolution really depend on chance? This is the key question. The principle that chance underpins evolution would appear to eliminate any possibility of intelligence or design. But does it? It all depends on how we view chance. Scientists place great emphasis on chance. They view many events as completely random and haphazard. Most scientists believe that apparent chance and randomness in physics and biology makes the idea of a creation completely redundant. But could this reflect a limited understanding of chance?

Imagine for a moment that there really were supernatural beings quietly at work behind the scenes in nature. Their interventions might appear to us to be random accidents. Seeing no material cause operating, we would probably conclude that such events were pure chance, with no pattern behind them. It is the story of the chickens in the garden again. To the chickens, there would be much that seemed to happen more or less at random. They know that food appears at some point, but they have no way of predicting precisely when. Likewise their eggs vanish but they don't understand why. The philosophers among them might say that it is all a very hit and miss affair. Yet the farmer knows when he is going to feed the chickens and the purpose for taking their eggs. To him there is no element of chance – apart from knowing how many eggs he will get!

What we see as chance depends upon our perspective. In the West, many things are put down to pure chance. In the East, by contrast, it is believed that what appears to be chance reveals the working of a greater order in the universe as a whole.

One example of this is the Eastern attitude to divination. Divination was treated with great respect throughout the ancient world. It was widely practised in the civilisations of ancient Greece and Rome; through it, the supernatural was believed to reveal itself in our world.

China is famous for a book of divination called the *I Ching*. In a foreword to one translation, Carl Jung wrote,

> The Chinese mind, as I see it at work in the I Ching, seems to be exclusively preoccupied with the chance aspect of events.
>
> What we call coincidence seems to be the chief concern of this peculiar mind and what we worship as causality passes almost unnoticed.

Like many other forms of divination, the *I Ching* involves the interpretation of a random series of events. Carl Jung said that in the old Chinese tradition, spiritual agencies were believed to act in a mysterious way behind the *I Ching*. Yet this ancient oracle, widely respected for its immense power, operates through chance.

In the West, it has been taken for granted that chance precludes the divine. However, in other cultures this is not always the case. American Indians and other aboriginal peoples are renowned for their awareness of chance. Through it, they perceive the supernatural operating even in the most trivial of circumstances.

What we perceive as chance may not be chance at all. Could it be the footprints of a higher intelligence at work in our world? When Einstein said "God does not play dice" he may have been wrong. It may well be that it is through dice that God plays.

It is natural to attribute something to chance when we don't perceive an underlying mechanism. Evolution is a fact. It is the mechanism of evolution that is in question – and whether or not there is intelligence at work behind it.

Biologists believe that evolution is driven by mutations. They believe that chance modifications of DNA lie at the heart of evolutionary change. This apparent randomness seems to eliminate any notion of a purpose or direction to evolution.

For a start, how could mutations be controlled? There would have to be some way in which intelligence could act on DNA. How would it operate? There would have to be some mechanism whereby purposeful changes could be introduced to DNA. What could it possibly be? Furthermore, the whole idea of purpose implies intelligence. Yet most biologists believe that intelligence has emerged through evolution. They see it as a consequence of life – not its cause. If there is intelligence behind evolution, everything is back to front. For a 'design' theory of evolution to make any sense, we would need to completely rethink the relationship between intelligence, life and mind.

The first clue to understanding how intelligence might act on DNA lies in some remarkable research findings from America. This work, conducted just before and after the Second World War, revealed mysterious and unexpected patterns of electrical activity in plant and animal forms.

Dr Harold Saxton Burr, Professor of Anatomy at Yale University, mounted an extensive programme of research to investigate this phenomenon. Burr made meticulous observations for a period of over twenty years from the mid 1930s to the late 1950s, and published over 50 papers on this subject in American medical and scientific journals.

Burr found minute electrical patterns in and on every living thing he tested, from leaves to newt eggs, and from human bodies to sprouting seeds. He had to use very sensitive equipment because the electrical patterns were very difficult to detect. It was as though he was measuring the shadow of something intangible. Burr called it the electro-dynamic field of life, the Life Field, or simply the L-field.

Burr explained this 'invisible and intangible' field as follows:

> Most people who have taken high-school science will remember that if iron-filings are scattered on a card held over a magnet they will arrange themselves in the pattern of the 'lines of force' of the magnet's field. And if the filings are thrown away and fresh ones scattered on the card, the new filings will assume the same pattern as the old.
>
> Something like this – though infinitely more complicated – happens in the human body. Its molecules and cells are constantly being torn apart and rebuilt with fresh material from the food we eat. But, thanks to the controlling L-field, the new molecules and cells are rebuilt as before and arrange themselves in the same pattern as the old ones . . .
>
> When we meet a friend we have not seen for six months there is not one molecule in his face which was there when we last saw him. But, thanks to his controlling L-field, the new molecules have fallen into the old, familiar pattern and we can recognise his face.
>
> Until modern instruments revealed the existence of the controlling L-fields, biologists were at a loss to explain how

Figure 22. Professor Harold Saxton Burr, with the vacuum tube microvoltmeter he developed to measure the Life Field

> our bodies 'keep in shape' through ceaseless metabolism and changes of material. Now the mystery has been solved: the electro-dynamic field of the body serves as a matrix or mould, which preserves the 'shape' or arrangement of any material poured into it, however often the material may be changed.

The most exciting aspect of Burr's work concerns a process called cellular differentiation. It is a mystery in biology how, from a single fertilised cell at conception, an organism can grow and develop. The cell repeatedly divides, millions upon millions of times, and each daughter cell has genetic material identical to the original fertilised ovum. The mystery is what tells one group of cells to be an eye, for example, and another group a leg. This process of the cells growing in different ways to form particular body tissues is called differentiation.

Burr used the L-field to propose a solution to the mystery of differentiation. He explained differentiation using the image of a jelly-mould:

> When a cook looks at a jelly-mould she knows the shape of the jelly she will turn out of it. In much the same way, inspection with instruments of an L-field in its initial stage can reveal the future 'shape' or arrangement of the materials it will mould. When the L-field in a frog's egg, for instance, is examined electrically it is possible to show the future location of the frog's nervous system because the frog's L-field is the matrix which will determine the form which will develop from the egg.

A distinguished friend of Burr commented,

> The growth and development of an embryo would seem to be the result of the fact that some kind of a factor sits on top of the embryo during its entire development and gives it direction.

According to Burr, the location of a cell in the L-field is as important as the genetic information it contains. The L-field is like an energy blueprint which directs each cell in its development into a specific type of tissue.

In the L-field, Burr believed that he had solved the mysteries of biological life. Most scientists, however, have rejected this conclusion. Burr's interpretation of his results is highly controv-

Figure 23. Kirlian photograph showing the energy field around a human hand

ersial because it implies that there is more to life than mere biochemistry. It calls into question the most sacred doctrines of modern biology by suggesting the existence of an independent life energy animating living organisms.

Many other scientists and philosophers have toyed with the idea of a life field associated with living organisms. In the 1920s, the term *elañ vital* was introduced by the so-called 'vitalist' philosophers to describe the animating principle behind life. Later, a biologist called Hans Driesch coined the name 'entelechy' to describe the guiding principle which controls the development of an embryo. In the 1960s and 70s, two Russian scientists, Semyon and Valentina Kirlian, developed a technique for taking vivid, colour photographs of the energy patterns of life.

Kirlian photography suggests that the life field persists even after the tissue is removed. For instance if a leaf is photographed, an energy pattern is still evident where a bit of leaf has been removed. The tissue has gone, but the life field for it seems to remain.

More recently, Rupert Sheldrake has postulated a 'morphogenetic' field, which he says is responsible for the form and development of living organisms.

Sheldrake uses the morphogenetic field to answer many questions about living things for which biological science has no adequate explanation. However, the concept of the morphogenetic field goes beyond that of the L-field, transcending space and time and existing beyond scientific measurement.

Furthermore, Sheldrake uses it to account for all organisation in the world, both animate and inanimate. Sheldrake envisages an ascending hierarchy of interlocking morphogenetic fields extending from sub-atomic particles through individual cells to the complete organism – and even beyond to the 'blueprints' of entire species.

The research by Burr, the evidence of Kirlian photography, and Sheldrake's hypothesis are all consistent with the idea that there is some form of energy which envelops and permeates living things. To Burr, the energy appeared to be related to electromagnetic fields. To Sheldrake, the fields involved in the order and organisation of living organisms are beyond physical measurement and outside space and time. The concept of super-energy can provide a new perspective on all these ideas.

It could be suggested that the true 'fields of life' are simply fields of *super-energy*. Physical bodies are always separated from one another by space, time or size. However energy and super-energy are not separated by these dimensions. It would therefore be possible for a field or body of super-energy to coincide with a physical body – that is, it could *coexist* with it in our world. The higher energy body could superimpose itself on the physical body, 'sitting on top of it' and interpenetrating it in just the way that Burr's colleague described.

Every living organism could have associated with it a body or field of super-energy by means of which its life processes are ordered. Such a super-energy field, of a different substance to matter and transcending our space and time, would correlate in many respects with Sheldrake's morphogenetic field. In its interaction with living organisms, it could be responsible for the electrical effects that Burr detected as the L-field.

In this way, the vortex could begin to offer a physical basis for a new science of life. Contemporary biology is based on a reductionist view of life. It teaches that life is a mere consequence of complex biochemical reactions occurring in living cells. But this materialistic doctrine leaves unanswered many questions about living things. The prime question is, what is life itself? Modern 'systems' thinkers would have us believe that life is merely a consequence of a set of processes. The new basis for biology proposed here sees life instead as the result of an independent reality manifesting through these processes.

This understanding suggests a new fundamental premise for biology – namely that life is a consequence of fields of super-energy. Biological life would be the result of a super-energy field super-imposed upon a physical body in our world, in such a way that a very special form of interaction is possible between them. This premise opens the door to providing new explanations for the organisation of living things. It is also crucial in explaining how intelligence could act to drive the evolutionary process.

But how would super-energy interact with living organisms? How could it be involved in evolution? As we have seen, matter si different in substance from super-energy. Super-energy would not normally interact with matter. Like radio waves, it is of a different 'stuff' to matter. It usually passes right through objects in our world. However, radio waves do interact with special forms of matter through a process called *resonance*. It is through resonance that super-energy could interact with matter.

The principle of resonance is very simple. If a tuning fork is sounded in a room containing a piano, each string on the piano tuned to the same pitch will start to vibrate. This is resonance. All the other strings, tuned to different notes, remain motionless. Through resonance, energy is transferred from the tuning fork to the string, causing it to vibrate.

Resonance is the key to the interaction of super-energy with matter. Consider a radio. Radio waves are subtle and don't interact with bricks and mortar. However, if a radio is tuned to the radio waves, then suddenly the home is filled with voices and music. Radio waves have little effect on the matter of the building, but a considerable effect on the matter in a radio set. The radio contains a tuned coil which resonates to the radio waves that sweep through it. As they do so, the vibrations in the radio waves are transferred to the coil. These vibrations are then amplified and transformed into sound in the loudspeaker.

In nature there is a very similar resonant form. Within all living organisms there is a structure that could conceivably receive vibrations from the subtle fields of super-energy. This resonant form is within the nucleus of every cell. It is DNA itself.

The DNA molecule was shown by Crick and Watson to have a double helix structure. This double helix is then coiled repeatedly upon itself – forming a coil reminiscent of that in a television set or radio. The DNA molecule, acting as a resonant coil, could receive vibrations from a field of super-energy. In this way, DNA could bridge the gap between the super-physical world and our own.

This model begins to show how super-energy could be intimately involved in evolution and the essential processes of life. To date, biologists have researched the chemistry of DNA without considering the full implications of its physical structure. Understanding DNA as a resonant form could open a whole new vista in biology, based on a principle which could be called *DNA resonance*. This interaction between super-energy and living organisms could be the secret of life.

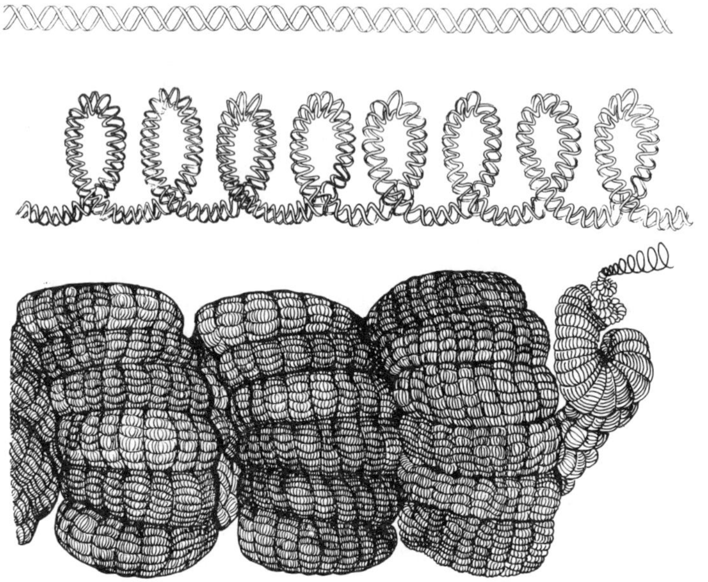

Figure 24. The DNA molecule is a double helix which is repeatedly wound on itself, forming a complex structure highly reminiscent of an electrical coil

Biologists believe that DNA is the secret of life. However they focus only on its chemical structure. We are suggesting that the physical structure of DNA may be just as important. The physical properties of DNA may be just as vital as its chemistry. It could be that DNA has the double function, in its chemical structure, to carry the genetic codes, and in its physical structure, to resonate to the vibrations in the super-energy field.

Theorists such as Sheldrake are convinced that the high degree of organisation in organisms cannot be reduced to the properties of their individual cells, that the whole is not just the sum of its constituent parts.

But they have been unable to point to any physical organising principle or mechanism. DNA resonance is a physical process whereby information for the ordering of biological life could be communicated to the heart of every cell.

Consider, for example, how DNA resonance might be used to control the mysterious process of differentiation. This process is critical to many living organisms. It is crucial to the development of a multicellular animal from an embryo.

Immediately after conception, all the cells are identical; the embryo is just an undifferentiated bundle of cells. Very soon, however, the cells begin to change. One group of cells develops into an eye, another into a brain, and yet others into limbs, heart and other essential organs. The question is, what brings about these changes? The DNA in each cell is identical; at this stage, every single cell has the potential to become virtually any cell in the body.

How then does each cell develop into a differentiated, specialised structure?

We have already suggested that the super-energy field could transmit to the DNA molecule in a way analogous to radio. Clearly the programme being transmitted via DNA resonance would not be sound and music! What if it were more like a computer program? A computer program is a set of instructions. It could convey information for guiding life processes. In the process of differentiation, each cell could be acting like a 'radio-computer', receiving and following instructions transmitted to it by the super-energy field. At each stage of the embryo's development, different instructions would be transmitted. The cells would follow the instructions in each phase of the program, until their development was complete. We could call this set of instructions a *Life-program.*

In this analogy, the Life-program corresponds to computer software; the cells are equivalent to computer hardware. Without software, this hardware is just a mass of undifferentiated tissue. Under the control of the software, the cells can grow in their own specialised way.

Each cell would receive a Life-program directing the course of its development within the tissue of which it is a part. This in its turn would be part of the Life-program for the organism as a whole. It would be rather like constructing a huge, immensely complex machine from a series of blueprints each corresponding to an ever-increasing level of organisation.

It is easy to see how the development of a cell could be controlled by the Life-program. DNA is ultimately responsible for everything that happens in the cell – including its structure, differentiation, and reproduction. All the basic information is contained in the DNA of each cell. It is all a matter of which section of the DNA molecule is read out – which group of genes is switched on or off. It is just like video editing. When a video is edited, sections are either used or ignored in order to create an edited copy. In the cell a similar process occurs. Its development depends upon which sections of its DNA are utilised and which are ignored. The idea is that the Life-program – originating in the super-energy field and transmitted to the heart of the cell via DNA resonance – would be directing this process.

These new concepts point to a mechanism whereby intelligence could guide evolution. The key lies in the new role we have ascribed to DNA. A change in the Life-program could modify the chemical structure of DNA and so alter the genetic codes. These design changes in the genes of an organism would appear as variations in its offspring. In this way the Life-program could be used to control evolution.

Alternatively, if evolutionary change is more a question of selecting the read-out of new sections of existing DNA, it is clear that the Life-program again offers a credible mechanism. It may well be that both processes are vital in the creation of a new species. In some cases, it may be necessary to create new genetic material. In others, it may be sufficient to draw on the pool of existing material, exploiting in a new way what is already there. In either case, it is clear that the Life-program could control what is happening.

It may be that the Life-program normally acts to preserve the chemical structure of DNA during its replications. DNA is remarkable in that in the course of billions of replications only one or two errors occur. The Life-program may have a role to play in the checking and correcting mechanisms responsible for DNA's remarkable accuracy and fidelity in handling information. This is precisely the kind of task at which a computer program excels.

If DNA is crucial to life processes, one might ask how DNA itself came to be formed. How could the Life-program begin to operate without DNA? The answer may lie in crystals. Biologists speculate that complex self-replicating organic molecules such as DNA could have evolved from simple crystals.

Crystals are capable of self-replication. Moreover, they are resonant forms and could conceivably respond to vibrations in super-energy fields permeating them. Crystals – with their dual capability of self-replication and resonance – are the obvious candidates to be the precursors of life.

Biology has baulked at the idea of purpose and intelligence behind evolution. In the absence of a mechanism for directing genetic variation, it has been forced to conclude that mutation is an entirely random process. By contrast, the picture we have painted shows how mutations could be deliberately induced. It becomes easy to see how genetic variation could be under intelligent control. Creative hands could be shaping life on Earth, via DNA resonance.

Intelligent forces could be reaching into our world – penetrating to the heart of every living cell, to alter genetic codes. They could be purposefully adapting species to changing circumstances – equipping their offspring to exploit new opportunities.

DNA resonance, then, offers an underlying mechanism through which evolution could be directed by outside intelligence. But what could this intelligence be?

Most biologists argue that intelligence and the mind are consequences of neuro-physiology, by-products of the complex chemical reactions going on inside living organisms. They believe that life, mind and intelligence have themselves evolved out of chaos through the instrumentation of nothing but blind chance acted on by the process of natural selection.

The alternative view is that mind and intelligence are universal principles that have an independent existence – that they manifest through biological life rather than arise from it. This would imply that they are the cause rather than the consequence of life. As first principles, mind and intelligence would have created the vehicles in which they are now embodied on Earth.

It could be that some 'universal mind' operates throughout the living world, guiding the progress of life on Earth. The Life-programs themselves might be thoughts, originating in this universal mind. Living cells, acting like radio sets, might be receiving signals from intelligent sources in the higher realms of the universe. These thought-form signals, resonating with DNA molecules, would be translated into changing genetic codes. Universal intelligence could in this way be directing the process of biological evolution towards increased order and diversity.

In the higher realms, there could be a whole hierarchy of intelligent beings acting like managers of evolution, forming, as it were, a 'celestial civil service'.

Who is to say that it might not include the legendary Pan – together with a host of nature spirits, devas and the like – all working in harmony with the universal mind?

In Pan, we can see the image of a god guiding evolution through resonance. Pan is depicted as playing on pipes. The tune he sounds could be imagined as the Life-program. The sequence of notes resonating through his pipes might be seen as setting up the sequence of genetic codes of DNA. As Pan continues to play the same tune, DNA remains the same and species are unaltered. However, when Pan pipes a new tune, DNA codes are changed and a new species emerges.

Evolution, as we see it, may be the tool of creation. Universal intelligence might not be following a pre-ordained plan. It may be learning from the multitude of experiences of life. Intelligence could be experimenting with new life forms. Earth would be the testing ground for new biological models, where designs are monitored and progressively refined. It would be rather like the development of electronic equipment by human engineers. Radio sets have evolved over the years from the crude 'cat's whisker' crystal set to the modern hi-fi stereo tuner. Natural selection could be compared to the open market, where new brands of equipment are tried and tested; the good ones succeed and the poor ones fail.

The 'gods' may be scientists. Working by trial, error and experiment, they could be developing life on Earth much as we develop technology. There need be no conflict between creation and evolution. It might be precisely through evolution that the gods have created life on Earth. Evolution and creation are totally compatible. It could be that the natural world, as the handiwork of the gods, is a masterpiece of genetic engineering!

CHAPTER 11

The Many Bodies of Man

Imagine you are in a building when a fire breaks out. The fire alarm sounds and the noise of it is deafening. You phone for the fire brigade and within minutes firemen arrive. But to your horror all they do is rush in with their axes and chop through the cables to the fire alarm, silencing it. They pat you on the back and shake you by the hand, saying, "I am sure you feel better now that the dreadful noise has stopped!". Then they disappear into the night leaving the fire raging.

Such firemen would be considered totally irresponsible by almost everyone. Yet we ourselves behave like this all the time. It has become commonplace for us to treat the symptoms of disease, rather than the root causes. For example, if we have a migraine or an attack of arthritis we probably take a couple of aspirin or ask our doctor to prescribe some other pain-killing drug. Pain is a symptom of disease. It is equivalent to an alarm bell warning that something is amiss in the body. To suppress the symptoms of a disease without tracing and correcting its root cause is as stupid as cutting off a fire alarm without extinguishing the fire.

This symptomatic approach cannot be blamed on the doctors. We put them under great pressure as we seek immediate alleviation of symptoms – an instant cure that requires no effort on our part.

More and more people – and many doctors – now recognise the limitations of this symptomatic approach in orthodox medicine. Many common ailments have been labelled as incurable and their symptoms are suppressed with drugs which have a spectrum of nasty side-effects. Over-worked doctors have precious little time, which causes as much distress to them as it does to their patients.

Today there is a rapid increase in the number of doctors who recognise the value of complementary therapies. But still many ordinary people find it difficult to accept alternative medicine. To begin with, it usually requires that they make some effort to heal themselves by examining and, where necessary, changing, their attitudes, lifestyle and diet. Furthermore, whilst most people accept that alternative medicine works, nobody seems to understand why.

To Western medical science, the principles underlying complementary therapies are often baffling. This has been clearly stated by the medical profession itself. In England, the growing popularity of alternative medicine prompted the British Medical Association to set up a committee to investigate it. The committee's secretary made clear its difficulty in a statement issued before the committee started work. Commenting on two examples of alternative practices, osteopathy and reflexology, he said,

> While osteopathy appears to be a series of skills that can be exercised to relieve conditions that we can understand, I have much greater difficulty in accepting the philosophical basis of other therapies of which reflexology appears to be a good example . . . I think it is unlikely that the working party will be able to give great credibility to the ideas that underline reflex zone therapy of the feet. Indeed I think it is likely that we shall positively reject the philosophical basis of this therapy.

Many people, including doctors, feel a deep sense of frustration at this situation. Medicine is, after all, an empirically-based practice. Why should it have to reject a therapy out of hand because of its philosophy – because the ideas behind it do not conform to the contemporary theories of medical science? Surely a practice should be accepted or rejected on the basis of its results?

Medical researchers with experiments that support complementary medicine can have a very hard time. Take for example the celebrated case of Professor Benveniste, a medical researcher in France. When he devised a laboratory experiment which appeared to show that homoeopathy really worked, a scientific witch-hunt ensued. A team of scientific 'ghostbusters', including a stage magician, descended on his laboratory outside Paris. For Benveniste, it was like a visit from the inquisition. His lab was turned upside down and his records were pulled apart. The team was determined to show that his results were fake. How could these homoeopathic effects possibly be real when they flew in the face of all physical theory?

There is a real need for an explanation of alternative or complementary medicine to enable us to understand how and why it works. Many practices are still very difficult to accept because they have no explanation in science. A coherent and unified theory for alternative medicine could help to make it far more acceptable not only to orthodox medical science but to all of us.

In complementary medicine, there are many different therapies employing a wide variety of techniques. However, there is a key principle which most of them share – the recognition of an invisible energy in and around the body which is essential to its integrity and well-being. Alternative practitioners talk of an 'energy' body, surrounding and permeating the physical body. Some of them refer to an 'etheric' body, others call it a 'subtle' or 'sensitive' body.

Many of the otherwise incomprehensible and sometimes bizarre treatments in alternative medicine claim to operate on this energy body.

The energy body is said to act as a blueprint for the physical form, influencing its processes and functions. Alternative practitioners claim that if the energy body is treated, the physical body will heal itself.

In *acupuncture*, it is considered that there are definite flow lines in the energy body called 'meridians'. Each organ in the physical body is said to be surrounded by a pool of subtle energy. The meridians act like streams, connecting the pools of energy deep within the body to the peripheral areas of the skin. An acupuncturist treats the organs through the meridians.

He stimulates or sedates the flow of energy in the meridian according to his diagnosis of the energy state of the organ concerned. He does this by inserting needles into the appropriate meridians at strategic acupuncture points. In this way, acupuncture seeks to harmonise and balance the energy body, encouraging the physical body to heal itself.

Reflexology is based on the principle that blocks in the energy body can be released by massaging the soles of the feet. Specific points on the feet are thought to correspond to particular organs.

By massaging the correct points, the reflexologist aims to rebalance the energy and stimulate healing in the appropriate organ. In the *metamorphic technique*, massage applied to the side of the foot is considered to harmonise the energy pattern of the body as whole.

Homoeopathy has its roots in the teachings of Hippocrates; it was established as a modern system of treatment by the German Dr Hahnemann at the end of the eighteenth century. Like acupuncture, homoeopathy regards illness as an imbalance in the underlying energy pattern or vital force of a person.

Homoeopaths administer remedies which are designed to resonate with this underlying energy, so as to harmonise it and stimulate healing.

Homoeopathy takes its name from the idea that 'like cures like'. According to Hahnemann, a substance which produces a set of symptoms in a healthy person will alleviate the same symptoms in a sick person. Following this principle, a homoeopath might, for example, administer an arsenic-based substance to someone with stomach disorder on the basis that arsenic causes stomach problems in a healthy person.

However, the homoeopath prescribing this remedy would not be administering arsenic in any significant amount. Homoeopathic remedies are prepared by a percussing and diluting procedure known as 'potentising'. In this process, a small amount of the original substance is diluted by mixing it with a quantity of inert material, such as fructose powder. The resulting mixture is beaten, or 'percussed'. This process is then repeated to produce successively greater 'potencies'. The most potent remedies have virtually none of the original chemical substance left within them. A potent arsenic remedy would contain barely a single atom of arsenic.

This example is an over-simplification. A homoeopath treats the whole person, not just particular symptoms. Deciding on a homoeopathic remedy is a more difficult task than prescribing a drug. In conventional medicine, symptoms are matched with an appropriate drug. A good homoeopath considers personality, emotions and overall body constitution, as well as the obvious symptoms presented. He will take these as pointers to the patient's underlying energy pattern and prescribe remedies designed to correct imbalances and blocks in the pattern as a whole.

Alternative practitioners are generally united in the belief that some sort of subtle energy exists which has a profound effect upon the physical body. But if there are subtle energies associated with the physical body, what could these energies be?

In the light of the previous chapter, it would seem natural to assume that these subtle energies are fields of *super-energy*. The energy body referred to by alternative practitioners might simply be a body of super-energy interpenetrating the physical body. In this way, the idea of super-energy could provide a rational basis for alternative medicine as an integral part of a new world view.

Previous attempts by science to understand alternative medicine have baulked at its concept of energy. Alternative practitioners speak of 'life energy' as though it were some kind of real substance which permeates living organisms. Science, on the other hand, defines energy as a measure of activity and change. Some scientists have attempted to reconcile this conflict by treating the 'energy body' as merely a metaphor describing the dynamic patterns of self-organisation within an organism. Using modern 'systems' thinking they have attempted to explain away the energy body as nothing more than a concept with no underlying reality.

The vortex lends support to the alternative view that energy has an independent reality. From this, it can be supposed that the energy body has a reality independent of life systems and could itself be the first cause of life. Since Einstein, physics has come to recognise that energy is the only basic reality in our world. Through the vortex it has been possible to show *how* matter is a form of energy. This new understanding has shown that the substance of matter itself is merely movement, that is, activity and change. Matter may appear to be more real than an intangible field of energy but in fact, the ephemeral fields of life energy, invisible to our senses, could be quite as real as matter. Alternative practitioners may be entirely correct in treating them as such.

The concept of super-energy removes the stumbling block of an intangible life field. It points to the possibility of forms of energy existing beyond the physical world. It also explains how such a life energy field could permeate and interpenetrate a physical body. A field of super-energy could 'coincide' with a physical body because there is no space-time separation between energy and super-energy.

The concept of super-energy provides a theoretical foundation for alternative medicine. Alternative medicine has previously been regarded as unscientific. However, from the new perspective, it is the materialistic foundations of conventional medicine which should be dismissed, not the philosophy behind alternative medicine. Alternative practitioners could indeed be operating on an intangible body of energy just as they claim. Alternative medicine is widely regarded as 'energy medicine', but we can only understand this view when we fully comprehend the meaning of energy. It requires a revolution in physics to enable science to embrace the reality of alternative medicine.

The new ideas of energy not only lead to a clearer understanding of the principles behind alternative medicine, they also clarify many of its practices. Take homoeopathy for instance. Homoeopathy could be understood by realising that its remedies act on the energy body rather than on the body chemistry. The potentisation process by which they are prepared can be compared with the process of taking an impression. Imagine putting your foot into a bucket of plaster. When you take it out, it leaves an impression in the plaster. Your foot could be described as the positive and the impression as the negative. In homoeopathy, the energy pattern associated with the original chemical represents the 'positive' from which an impression is to be made. In the process of percussion and dilution, the energy pattern associated with the chemical is 'impressed' onto the inert substrate material, forming a 'negative'. With continued potentisation, the energy negative is 'enlarged', whereas the concentration of the original chemical, the positive, is vastly reduced. It is as if the impression of the foot in the plaster has been reproduced millions of time, whereas the foot has been completely removed.

When the remedy is taken, the enlarged negative image is projected onto the patient's energy body, brightening up the dull spots and toning down the highlights. In a physical sense this could be understood as two opposite wave vibrations cancelling each other out in the process known to physics as interference. The result would be to reduce excesses and make up deficiencies in the patient's energy pattern. It is impossible to make sense of homoeopathy in terms of chemistry, but it begins to make sense in terms of physics.

Homoeopathy is said to be based on the underlying principle that 'like cures like'. But this new account paints a slightly different picture. In potentisation, it is an energy negative which is produced and then amplified.

The remedy could be thought of as holding a 'key' which unlocks a blockage in the super-energy of the body. This new account of homoeopathy would bring it more into line with orthodox biological science. Biochemistry recognises this type of 'lock and key' mechanism operating in many life processes, from the interaction between anti-bodies and viruses to the replication of protein from RNA.

Homoeopathy is only one of a number of alternative practices that can be understood in terms of the physics of super-energy. Take *radionics* for example. Practitioners of radionics diagnose and treat their patients using instruments based on electrical coils and condensers. It could be that these instruments allow them to *tune in* to the resonant frequencies of a patient's super-energy field. Practitioners claim to recognise specific frequencies corresponding to particular organs and diseases, which can be treated by harmonising and correcting the inappropriate vibrations. Some radionics instruments are said to 'broadcast' wave patterns which cancel out those of a specific disease. This could be the result of an interference process similar to that we have described for homoeopathy. In radionics instruments, the coils and condensers are not connected in a normal electrical circuit; they interact directly with the super-energy field by resonance.

Medical dowsing, sometimes called *radiesthesia*, can also be understood in terms of resonance. In radiesthesia, a pendulum is used to indicate changes in the patient's energy field. There is an interaction between the super-energy field of the practitioner and that of the patient. The practitioner's energy field resonates to that of the patient. It is as if he or she acts as a life energy *meter*; the pendulum could be viewed as the needle on the meter.

Changes in the energy body can also be detected by changes in muscle tone. This is the basis of *applied kinesiology* – the diagnostic system based on muscle testing.

Medical dowsing and muscle testing are primarily systems of diagnosis. They can also be used to identify the most beneficial therapy for a particular patient, establishing not only, for instance, the best herbal or homoeopathic remedy, but also the optimum dose.

Some people claim that the Earth itself has an energy body, with energy flow lines akin to acupuncture meridians in the human body. If this is so, it could explain phenomena such as ley lines and the Curry grid, a supposed network of energy lines spanning the entire globe. Dowsers can detect anomalies in this system, possibly via the interaction of their own super-energy body with that of the Earth. 'Negative' nodes in this network have been found by dowsers to correlate with the incidence of illness in people living over them, the strongest correlation being with cancer. It could be that such 'geopathic stress' causes its effects by depleting the human super-energy field.

Healing is one of the least understood and yet most powerful forms of alternative therapy. Healers appear to do little more than place their hands upon the patient or move them about nearby. They rarely have any form of medical training and baffle medical science by curing cancer and other chronic diseases without any knowledge of the conditions they are treating.

Healing is a therapeutic interaction between the super-energy body of the practitioner and that of the patient, without the intervention of any instruments or remedies. Healing may work by a process of resonance that acts to reinforce the body's energy blueprint. The process of balancing and removing blocks would permit a flow of 'healing' energy – supporting the renewal of cells and the growth of new and healthy tissue. In this way, healing would counteract disease wherever it occurs in the body. Self-healing is a characteristic of all living things; healing merely stimulates this natural process.

Healers talk, not of an energy body, but of an aura. Those who claim to see it describe it as full of colour, surrounding and permeating the physical body. Healers attach great importance to the aura; many say that it reacts almost immediately to changes in thought or feeling and to changes in the environment. They also claim that damage is visible in the aura some months before it shows itself in the physical body as disease.

This is very similar to what Professor Burr found in his research on the L-field. Burr used special voltmeters and electrodes to investigate electrical patterns on different parts of the body. He discovered that distortions in these electrical patterns gave an early indication of the onset of disease and in particular the onset of cancer.

Burr imagined the L-field as a jelly-mould, shaping and containing the physical body. He explained the early diagnosis of disease in terms of this image:

> When [the cook] uses a battered mould she expects to find some dents or bulges in the jelly. Similarly, a 'battered' L-field – that is, one with abnormal voltage-patterns – can give warning of something 'out of shape' in the body, sometimes in advance of actual symptoms.
>
> For example, malignancy in the ovary (and cervix) has been revealed by L-field measurements before any clinical sign could be observed. Such measurements, therefore, could help doctors to detect cancer early, when there is a better chance of treating it successfully.

To understand cancer, we need to consider more fully the role of super-energy in the vital processes of living organisms. In a multicellular organism, the foremost of these processes is cellular differentiation.

If a group of cells is extracted from an animal and grown in a petri dish they do not grow into a clone of the animal; instead they grow into an undifferentiated mass of tissue, a tumour. If these tumorous cells are then introduced back into the animal, they develop into cancer. Scientists have actually given mice cancer by removing liver cells, growing them in the laboratory, and then re-introducing them as tumours into the mice. It would seem that outside the influence of the super-energy body, cells have no blueprint for differentiation. This may well be the key to understanding cancer.

Any weakness in the body's blueprint would enable some cells to regress and grow into an undifferentiated mass, a cancerous tumour. It could be that Burr's L-field is a physical reflection of the inaccessible super-energy field. Perhaps there is a resonance effect, such that weakness in the super-energy field shows up in the electrical patterns of the body. This would explain why Burr noticed dramatic changes in his L-field in cases of cancer.

If distortions in electrical patterns point to abnormalities in the super-energy field, then measurements of body electricity could lead to a breakthrough in the early diagnosis of cancer. Burr's discovery of dramatic changes in the L-field preceding the emergence of clinical symptoms in cases of cancer has been verified by subsequent, independent scientific research. A team from the Department of Obstetrics and Gynaecology of the New York University College of Medicine investigated changes in the L-field in cases of cervical cancer and confirmed that these changes give an early indication of the onset of the disease. Despite this, Burr's extensive work has never been generally accepted by the medical establishment. This inexpensive, electronic method of giving an early warning of cervical cancer has been known since the war. However, it is still not available in hospitals or health clinics because the principles behind it do not conform to the materialistic world view of medical science.

What would weaken the life field and so predispose us to cancer? In classical India and China, it was the traditional belief that the natural environment, including the air we breathe and the food we eat, was charged with life energy – called *prana* in India and *ch'i* in China. It could be that in order to stay healthy we need life energy from these sources. Perhaps in some way we are nourished by life energy from our environment, our food and the air we breathe. Cancer was rare in primitive societies, where people lived close to the land. It is only in modern industrial society that cancer has become an epidemic.

The destruction of the natural environment has now become a cause of grave concern to many people. The tearing down of rain forests, the replacement of green meadows with industrial plant, towns and motorways, along with the gathering impact of pollution, are all causing alarm. People are well aware of the harmful effects of our industrial society at a physical level. However, it could be that industrialisation, pollution and increased urbanisation, are threatening us in far more insidious ways than we at present realise.

To begin with, by the destruction of the natural environment we may be destroying essential sources of life energy. In this manner, we may be denying ourselves vitality that we would otherwise obtain from the natural world. For example, it has been shown that in processed food the life energy is depleted; subjected to Kirlian photography, it shows practically no life field pattern.

Furthermore, on the physical principle that energy flows from a higher to a lower level, it may be that the devitalised environment and food actually deplete us, becoming charged up with life energy at our expense. The human energy body appears to be further weakened by electromagnetic pollution. Is it any wonder that there is an epidemic of cancer in industrial society?

It seems unlikely that these factors cause cancer directly. It is more likely that they increase our susceptibility to it. Exposed as we are to so many actual carcinogens, cancer would frequently follow. In a low energy state, the physical body may well be more vulnerable to toxins, viruses and diseases of all types, appearing almost to attract them to it. In a high energy state, when the super-energy body is strong and well-balanced, the physical body could by contrast be far more resilient, shrugging off and rejecting the effects of pollution, carcinogens and harmful bacteria.

Healers and practitioners of radionics and radiesthesia often claim to be able to diagnose and treat cancer and other diseases at a distance. This faculty, usually called *absent healing*, could be understood if the healer is not operating on the physical body directly but on the super-energy body which transcends our space and time. The doctor has to drive in his car to go out and treat a patient. But the laws governing super-physical interactions appear to be different. The evidence suggests that separation can be overcome by will or intention. The healer and the patient may be separated by thousands of miles, but merely by thought they can immediately be connected.

The separation of two people in the physical world does not mean that they are out of touch at a super-physical level. Even though they are far apart, their super-energy fields might be attuned at the level of mind and emotions by their love and continual thoughts for each other. Likewise, physical proximity between two people does not necessarily mean that their energy fields are connected. Strangers sitting next to each other in a crowded railway carriage, having no mental or emotional contact, could be totally separate in the realm of super-energy. They would be, as it were, on a totally different wavelength.

Healers and practitioners of radionics and radiesthesia very often use a 'witness' to facilitate this linking process. Any object imbued with the life energy of the patient can be used as a witness. Witnesses range from blood spots and hair samples to photographs, clothes and objects commonly handled by the patient. In *psychometry*, a person tunes into the entire past and present experience of another via contact with a witness of this kind.

Certain objects and places appear to have a special super-energy 'imprint' associated with them that arises from their exceptional history. An outstanding example of this phenomenon relates to the Roman spear of Longinus, which is part of the Habsburg treasure in Vienna, and is purported to have been used to pierce the side of Christ on the cross. Many world-dominating figures down through the ages are said to have had this object in their possession as a talisman of power. In his account of the occult background to the Second World War, Trevor Ravenscroft claimed that Hitler annexed Austria partly to gain possession of this artefact. It is said that he tuned into the energies associated with this spear and drew power from its extraordinary history.

The power to tune into the super-energy pattern related to an object or a person, underlies clairvoyance. A *clairvoyant* is someone who has this ability to a high degree. He or she is able to transcend space and time intuitively to read the energy pattern of past, present and future associated with an object, person or place. It is not that the future is immutable, but rather that the energy pattern built up in the past sets up a probability pattern predisposing future events. This pattern is not a certainty, it is more a propensity. Descrying the future in this way is similar to healers discerning an imbalance in the aura and, from it, predicting the onset of disease.

Clairvoyance is not restricted to a few gifted individuals. In reality we all have this ability to some extent. For example, we all make a link with anyone we choose, at an energy level, merely by calling them to mind. It should not come as a surprise when we find ourselves thinking of someone just before they phone. In such cases, our minds have simply made the connection first.

The truth is that mind is far greater than we usually appreciate. Many scientists believe that mind is a mere consequence of the brain. They like to imagine the brain as a computer and thoughts as the result of its activity. This notion makes clairvoyance, ESP and telepathy very hard to understand.

The evidence of clairvoyance and other parapsychological phenomena suggests that mind extends beyond the brain. In some people, it appears to reach into whole dimensions of the universe of which most of us are unaware.

Aldous Huxley suggested that the brain acts as a reducing valve on mind, an idea that he came to through his own experiences and the influence of the philosopher, C D Broad. In his book *The Doors of Perception*, Huxley quotes Broad as saying,

> Each person is at each moment capable of remembering all that has ever happened to him and of perceiving everything that is happening everywhere in the universe.

Broad believed that the role of the brain is to protect us from being overwhelmed and confused by this mass of knowledge, shutting out most of it, and leaving only what is necessary for our practical everyday life on Earth. In other words, he saw the function of the brain as being mainly eliminative and not productive. Huxley concurred with this view, saying "the brain does not *produce* mind, it *reduces* mind". As he put it,

> . . . each one of us is potentially Mind at Large. But in so far as we are animals, our business is at all costs to survive. To make biological survival possible, Mind at Large has to be funnelled through the reducing valve of the brain and nervous system. What comes out at the other end is a measly trickle of the kind of consciousness which will help us to stay alive on the surface of this particular planet . . . The various 'other worlds' with which human beings erratically make contact are so many elements in the totality of the awareness belonging to Mind at Large. Most people, most of the time, know only what comes through the reducing valve and is consecrated as real by the local language. Certain persons, however, seem to be born with a kind of by-pass that circumvents the reducing valve.

People often speak of man being made of a body and a mind two separate entities that are somehow joined together. Body and mind have each been taken to be the personal property of the individual. Each of us has a physical body that is completely personal to us. We are familiar with this box of bones and blood, bounded by the skin. We are inclined to think of the mind as bounded and boxed up in much the same way. We imagine it as a body of thoughts, memories and feelings which is personal to the individual in the same way as the physical body.

Huxley, however, does not speak of an individual mind. He saw mind more as something universal to which the brain gives us access. The brain could be compared to a television set. A television requires two things in order to operate: electrical power and programmes. Neither belongs to the individual set. The electrical power is something more universal that is fed in from the mains. The programmes are also external to the set. They come in from outside, as broadcasts or pre-recorded videos. The set merely allows us to choose which programme is displayed.

Mind is the conjunction of consciousness and thought. Consciousness is represented in the television analogy by mains power. Just as mains electricity is common to all receivers connected to the one national grid, it may be a common consciousness that empowers all brains. Thoughts would correspond to television programmes. Some are public – broadcasts or recordings borrowed from a video library. Others are private – creations of the home video camera. In the same way, some thoughts may originate in the brain, like home video creations, while others may be received from outside, like external programmes.

This analogy suggests that two things would be vital for conscious experience: consciousness itself and the objects of experience – thoughts, emotions and sensations. It is the conjunction of consciousness and thought – power and programme – that would give rise to individual experience.

But what is thought, and how could it exist outside the brain? Consider the television analogy again. Television programmes exist as electrical impulses in television sets. But they can also exist quite independently, as electromagnetic vibrations which radiate through space. Could the same be true of thought? We know that thought is associated with electrical impulses in the brain. Could thought also exist independently, for example as vibrations in the super-energy field?

If this were so, thought would have physical reality; it would be as real as matter or light. Furthermore, it is obvious that thought could exist beyond the brain; like electromagnetic waves, thoughts would be capable of radiating throughout the universe.

These suggestions are not absurd. There is considerable evidence that thought transcends the limits of the physical world. We often speak of 'the realm of thought' as being a world distinct from that of matter. Some people even say that thoughts travel faster than light. All of these ideas would make sense if thoughts were associated with super-energy vibrations in another realm of space and time.

It could be that the brain is an instrument capable of resonating to these vibrations. The brain, through some resonant structure in its neurophysiology, may mediate between super-energy and the physical world. If this is so, the brain could be a 'thought transceiver' – an instrument that transmits and receives thoughts, translating them into the physical world.

If thoughts are vibrations in the super-energy field, they could be transmitted via resonance direct from one super-energy field to another. In this way, thought-forms, like radio and television waves, could be broadcast throughout the universe. Thoughts, like broadcast radio signals, could be transmitted directly between people. The transmission of thought in this way would constitute telepathy.

Some of our thoughts appear to originate in our own heads, but others seem to pop up 'out of the blue'. We recognise this when we say such things as 'it just came to me' and 'it crossed my mind'. It would seem that we do not originate all of our thoughts. It is easy to make the mistake of identifying ourselves with our thinking, not realising that we receive rather than originate many of our thoughts. Some thoughts may be transmitted into the human psychosphere from higher realms of the universe; these might be considered to constitute the source of inspiration and genius.

When we think along a particular line, we notice that similar thoughts keep occurring to us. This could happen because we 'tune in' to resonate with a particular train of thought. It would be natural that we would then begin to receive any thoughts on that 'wavelength', which happen to be radiating in the psychosphere around us. This could account for the phenomenon Jung described as the 'collective unconscious'. If thoughts are intrinsically part of another realm, a realm of super-energy outside space and time, we could learn to pick them up from other places and times by tuning in properly. Understanding thought as a vibration can also help us to appreciate how resonant forms such as crystals might assist in this 'tuning' process, acting to store and amplify the vibrations.

Many people draw inspiration in their sleep, as reflected in the common statement 'I'll sleep on it'. If the greater part of mind exists beyond the brain, in sleep our consciousness could become aware of this greater reality beyond the physical realm. We may then awake, refreshed and enriched with other-worldly knowledge. This might account for some of our dreams.

Consciousness temporarily entering this greater reality of super-energy, not in sleep but in the waking state, could account for the phenomena of astral travelling and other out-of-the-body experiences.

These considerations cast a new light on memory. If thought can exist outside the brain, perhaps the same is true of memory. The brain is usually thought of as entirely responsible for storing memories. But could the greater part of our memory be held externally to it, as patterns in the super-energy field?

The brain is often compared to a computer. Every computer has a limited internal memory, but can access an unlimited amount of information stored externally on discs and tapes. In the same way, it may be that the brain only stores information required for immediate conscious activity. Far more information may be stored externally in the super-energy field – there to be accessed by the brain.

It is clear from hypnosis that the amount of information held in the human psyche is phenomenal. Perhaps the brain is tapping in to a potentially limitless memory bank in the super-energy field. In trance and in states of expanded consciousness, people seem to have access to transpersonal memory – as if they are visiting the public library, when normally they are restricted to their own shelf of books.

The idea that the brain is an instrument allowing access to

memory is supported by medical research. Studies of cases in which parts of the brain have been damaged or destroyed have failed to show that memories are located in any particular brain region. Rather, when the brain is damaged, or deteriorates with old age, the person's memory becomes fuzzy and unclear. The ability to access information is impaired. Perhaps all the information is still intact, but the physical process of tuning in to it no longer operates as well as it used to.

To conclude, fields of super-energy, surrounding and permeating the physical body, could constitute a higher energy body of man. Alternative medicine recognises the existence of a higher energy body which, acting as a blueprint, has a profound effect upon the physical body. In many alternative practices, healing effects are brought about by strengthening, harmonising and balancing this energy body – which may include working on the mind and emotions.

Alternative medicine recognises the physical reality of thought and the enormous part it has to play in the overall well-being of man. Negative thoughts and repressed emotions, as destructive vibrations in the energy body, can have detrimental effects on the physical body. The converse is also true.

Positive thoughts and emotions, harmonising the super-energy field, can heal the physical body. The effect of the mind on the body is, of course, recognised in orthodox medicine under the term 'psychosomatic'.

Many of the different types of alternative medical practice are sophistications of the basic art of healing. In all times there have been men and women of compassion, with a knowledge based on intuition rather than intellect, on experience rather than experiment. Very often these people have been natural healers. Healing is a legacy of wiser ages when a man was treated as a whole and unique person and the physical body was seen as an instrument serving a higher purpose. In sickness, the healer treated the whole person rather than just the symptoms of disease.

Jesus Christ was perhaps the greatest healer in recorded history. Christ, in resonance with the highest realms of the universe, may have tuned in to the life field of the stricken person at his feet. Through an intense stimulation of the super-energy blueprint, the body in his gaze could have been completely regenerated.

Teachers such as Christ were, of course, more concerned with healing the soul than the body. In ancient times, the soul was accorded greater significance than the body. Some people literally saw the soul as an aura, full of colour, which surrounded the body. This was sometimes portrayed as a halo. Charged with energy from the highest realms of the universe, the aura of the saint or mystic would appear – to one who could see it – to be full of brilliant and golden light.

The soul is generally taken to be an immaterial part of man that persists after death. It could be understood as made up of several super-energy fields. We have pictured the universe as a series of distinct realms of energy, each based on a different primal speed. The human energy body could have the same structure. Rather than being a single body of super-energy, it might consist of a series of distinct bodies, superimposed upon each other. In other words, each of us may have a whole ascending series of super-energy fields associated with his physical body. This would provide an explanation for the traditional esoteric idea of the many bodies of man. Such teachers as Rudolph Steiner, for example, described these subtle bodies as the *etheric* body, the *emotional* body, the *mental* body and the *astral* body.

We might envisage this ascending series of subtle bodies rather like successive layers of an onion, each one encapsulating the next.

In the many bodies of man, it is possible to see an echo of the structure of the universe as a whole as an ascending series of super-energy realms. We could look at the saying 'as above, so below' as expressing the idea that man's own make-up in this way reflects that of the universe. The vortex as a universal pattern is also evident in the energy body. Within the subtle bodies, people with psychic faculties see vortices of energy which have come to be known as *chakras*.

If every organism has at least some level of super-energy associated with it, then it could be said that not only man but every life form possesses a soul. Soul would occur wherever there is a field of super-energy: it would exist therefore at every level of biological life. Many people would accept that animals

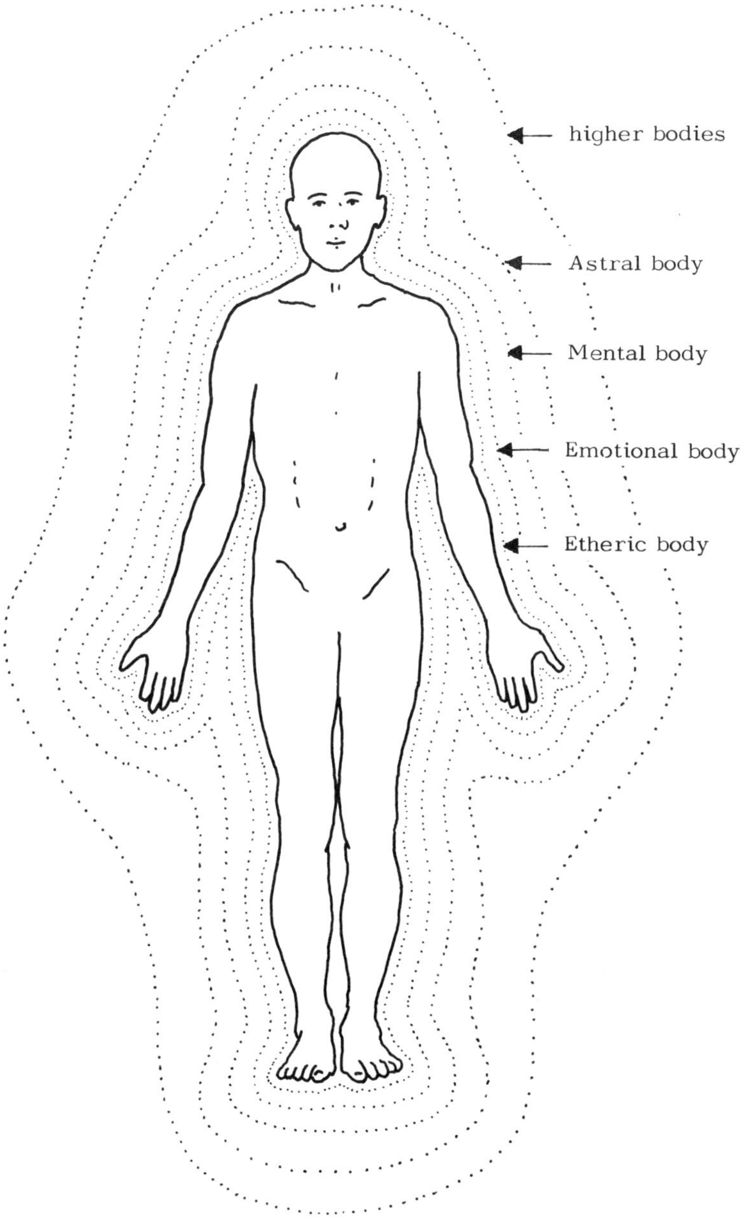

Figure 25. The higher energy fields are often depicted as a series of higher bodies surrounding and interpenetrating the physical body

and plants have some degree of awareness. If inanimate matter also had a field of super-energy associated with it – as Sheldrake assumes for the morphogenetic field – then even rocks and stones could have some basic level of soul consciousness associated with them. Many esoteric traditions, and aboriginal peoples, hold this to be so.

In the light of these understandings, it is easy to imagine that our personal consciousness could survive death and not be extinguished with the brain as many modern thinkers would have us believe. If thoughts and memories are attributes of the super-energy bodies, then the idea of their continuity beyond death is entirely reasonable. At death, the super-energy bodies would simply detach themselves from the physical body and cease to coexist with it.

This insight can free us from the fear of death which has haunted mankind down through the ages. A positive attitude to death is an integral aspect of the holistic approach to life.

CHAPTER 12

Lives after Death

The continuity of life after death is one of the most cherished of human beliefs. From time immemorial, people have been motivated by the idea of an after-life in another, quite different realm. This belief has usually focused on the existence of a permanent soul, an invisible part of a human being which survives death, taking the consciousness of the person into another world.

In Chapters 10 and 11, we proposed that every living organism has associated with it a super-energy body. This energy body – more akin to an energy field than a body of matter – confers life upon it. This super-energy body, perhaps consisting of an ascending series of fields, superimposes itself on the physical body, completely interpenetrating it. An organism would be alive when this body of super-energy is co-incident with it. Death would correspond to the state when this coexistence is terminated.

If it is true that the thoughts and memories of man are attributes of the super-energy body, then there is no reason to suppose that the personality would not continue after death. Released from the physical body, this higher body of man – which some might call the soul – would be free to return to its natural home in the higher, 'heavenly' realms of the universe. These ideas offer support to the idea of an after-life and challenge the notion that we are completely extinguished at death. At death, the vital principle that has animated the physical body simply leaves it to pursue a separate existence.

There is today an abundance of empirical evidence for survival after death. Literally thousands of purported after-death communications have been received via mediums and spiritualists, some of them passing stringent cross-checks which appear to establish their validity. For the purposes of this chapter, however, we have chosen to rely only on the accounts of people who are still alive. One important source of such evidence comes from research into near-death experiences –the reports of people brought back from the brink of death.

The number of people who have had a near-death experience has increased enormously thanks to medical developments in resuscitation. Today, doctors regularly 'bring back to life' people who have passed through clinical death.

It is now common practice to attempt resuscitation after a person has stopped breathing, even when their heart has stopped beating and all signs of life have ceased. The result is that many people are returning from death with extraordinary reports of an after-life.

One of the pioneering workers in this field was an American, Dr Raymond Moody. Moody collected hundreds of accounts of the experience of dying from people who had been resuscitated. Many of his subjects were people who had died in an accident or in hospital; doctors or other medically trained personnel had been at hand, or had arrived on the scene with resuscitation equipment, and had succeeded in bringing them back to life. The following accounts of the near-death experience are taken from Moody's description of his research in his book *Life after Life*.

Dr Moody found that, while everyone had a different experience, the reports contained many common elements. People appeared to be reporting different parts of a single underlying experience. Moody describes the early stages of the archetypal near-death experience as follows:

> A man is dying and, as he reaches the point of greatest physical distress, he hears himself pronounced dead by his doctor. He begins to hear an uncomfortable noise, a loud ringing or buzzing, and at the same time feels himself moving very rapidly through a long dark tunnel. After this, he suddenly finds himself outside of his own physical body, but still in the immediate physical environment, and he sees his own body from a distance, as though he is a spectator.

Some people were aware of looking down on their physical body, seeing it for example tangled in the wreck of a car or surrounded by distressed relatives or medical staff. Some people were baffled or confused at the state in which they found themselves. Others were quite clear about what had happened to them, as the following account illustrates:

> I thought that I was dead and I wasn't sorry that I was dead, but I just couldn't figure out where I was supposed to go. My thought and my consciousness were just like they are in life, but I just couldn't figure all this out. I kept thinking, 'Where am I going to go? What am I going to do?' and 'My god, I'm dead! I can't believe it!' Because you never really believe, I don't think, fully that you're going to die. It's always something that's going to happen to the other person, and although you know it you really never believe it deep down . .

Frequently people sought to reassure their doctors or relatives that they were not dead. However, they were quite unable to communicate with people around their bodies, who seemed not to hear them. One said,

> I saw them resuscitating me. It was really strange. I wasn't very high; it was almost like I was on a pedestal, but not above them to any great extent, just maybe looking over them. I tried talking to them but nobody could hear me, nobody would listen to me.

As Moody relates, when they came to terms with their odd condition, people usually noticed that they still had a body, but not at all like the physical one they had left behind. It had form, but no clear outline or colour. Some described it as a cloud and others as an energy field. They found themselves able to pass right through the people surrounding their dead body and through other objects in its vicinity. In this state, they were more aware of the thoughts of the people surrounding their physical bodies than of their voices and spoken words.
One woman said,

> I could see people all around, and I could understand what they were saying. I didn't hear them, audibly, like I'm hearing you. It was more like knowing what they were thinking, exactly what they were thinking, but only in my mind, not in their actual vocabulary. I would catch it the second before they opened their mouths to speak.

It would appear that in the near-death experience, people

enter a realm of mind quite separate from the physical body. That they seem to take their memory of places, people and things with them supports the idea that consciousness and memory can exist quite independently of the brain.

Another person reported:

> There was a lot of action going on, and people running around the ambulance. And whenever I would look at a person to wonder what they were thinking, it was like a zoom-up, exactly like through a zoom lens, and I was there. But it seemed that part of me – I'll call it my mind – was still where I had been, several yards away from my body. When I wanted to see someone at a distance, it seemed like part of me, kind of like a tracer, would go to that person. And it seemed to me at the time that if something happened any place in the world that I could just be there.

This report and others like it suggest that, when out of the body, we can move freely from one place to another simply by wishing to be there. The near-death experience in this way supports the idea that separation in the realms of super-energy can be overcome simply by will or intention.

Many people reported that their faculties of perception and awareness were heightened after death. That people can 'see' more clearly when they are out of the body make come as a surprise. Whilst we are alive in human bodies, we are aware of the physical world around us through sense organs. However, all these faculties, including the eyes, are left behind when we die. A person who is out of the body is obviously not seeing with the eyes or perceiving the world through any of the five senses.

In esoteric tradition it is said that the first subtle body is an exact counterpart of the physical body. This makes sense if it is a precise blueprint for the physical body. We could picture it as an 'etheric' jelly-mould with exactly the form of the body. This implies that it would have counterparts of the physical sense organs, such as the eyes. It could be that, inhabiting this body, we can actually see via waves of super-energy, perhaps some etheric counterpart to light.

A person in this transitional state would be aware not only of the physical world, but also the super-physical. Technically dead, he or she would be newly aware of the super-energy body quite separate from the physical body left behind. Now inhabiting a super-energy body, he or she would have the frustrating experience of being invisible to the doctors and relatives left behind, and unable to speak to them – while at the same time being able to read their minds. Being closer to the realm of thought, he or she would be able to perceive the thought-forms of their relatives more directly. This is borne out in the accounts.

The initial experience of dying was frequently described as distressing. Occasionally, it brought about a profound feeling of loneliness or depression.

However such feelings passed quickly as the experience developed. Some people were comforted by becoming aware of the presence of friends and relatives who had already died. These experiences are not a fantasy; in a number of cases, people have met relatives whom they did not know had died. Others progressed at once to what Dr Moody described as the most incredible feature common to most of the accounts he studied, namely the 'being of light'. In Dr Moody's words,

> Certainly the element which has the most profound effect on the individual is the encounter with a very bright light.
>
> Typically, at its first appearance this light is dim, but it rapidly gets brighter until it reaches an unearthly brilliance . . . not one person has expressed any doubt whatsoever that it was a being, a being of light. Not only that, it is a personal being. It has a very definite personality.
>
> The love and warmth which emanate from this being to the dying person are utterly beyond words, and he feels completely surrounded by and taken up in it, completely at ease and accepted in the presence of this being.

Normally, the being of light would then start to communicate with the dying person about his or her life. This communication was not through voice or language, but by direct transfer of thought. Moody summarised the typical course of the communication as follows:

> Usually the persons with whom I have talked try to formulate the thought into a question. Among the translations I have heard are: 'Are you prepared to die?', 'Are you ready to die?', 'What have you done with your life to show me?', 'What have you done with your life that is sufficient?' . . .

> all insist that this question, ultimate and profound as it may be in its emotional impact, is not at all asked in condemnation. The being, all seem to agree, does not direct the question to them to accuse them or to threaten them, for they still feel the total love and acceptance coming from the light, no matter what their answer may be. Rather, the point of the question seems to be to make them think about their lives, to draw them out.

This communication is often followed by the individual experiencing a rapid review of his or her life. Rather like a speeded-up slide show, everything is relived in a rapid succession of flickers. In some cases, the images are reported to be in vibrant colour, three-dimensional and even moving. From the most important to the most insignificant events, even the emotions and feelings of the time are experienced vividly and in chronological order as though every tiny detail has been stored in some vast memory bank.

One person described this life-review in the following way:

> This flashback was in the form of mental pictures, I would say, but they were much more vivid than normal ones. I saw only the high points, but it was so rapid it was like looking through a volume of my entire life and being able to do it within seconds. It just flashed before me like a motion picture that goes tremendously fast, yet I was fully able to see it, and able to comprehend it.

At this point, many individuals found that the being of light indicated that their time of death had not yet arrived, and that they were to return to the body. They then experienced themselves being drawn back into the body and waking up. Others experienced something like a lake or mist which they began to cross. On the other side, they saw people beckoning to them, but they never completed the crossing and found themselves returned to the body.

Many people experienced a strong desire to return to the body on first leaving it, especially during the phase of depression or loneliness. However after encountering the light, most lost their desire to return to the physical body. They wanted to remain in the presence of the light. But some made a definite decision to return:

> It was wonderful over there on the other side, and I kind of wanted to stay. But knowing that I had something good to do on Earth was just as wonderful in a way. So, I was thinking, 'Yes, I must go back and live', and I got back into my physical body. I almost feel as though I stopped the bleeding myself. At any rate, I began to recover after that.

None of Moody's subjects found death a frightening experience, except for those attempting suicide. These people found that the distress they were attempting to escape from lived on with them. Coupled with an intense regret at taking their own life, death was for them a continuation of their suffering rather than a relief.

Death by natural means was on the contrary experienced as a deliverance. Some people described it as a homecoming or an awakening. Others talked about a graduation or even an escape from jail. Many were sorry to find themselves back in the body again.

Those brought back from the dead feel that they have been granted a profound illumination. Often they say that it has helped them to find a deeper meaning to their lives. Almost invariably they lose the fear of death which haunts so many people.

Accounts of the near-death experience strongly suggest that consciousness, thoughts, memories and emotions survive physical death. The fact that these faculties appear to survive death could be taken to indicate that they belong to the super-energy body rather than to the physical body. The near-death experience supports the idea that consciousness and thought have a reality independent from the brain and nervous system – that they are not, as science supposes, mere consequences of human neurophysiology that are extinguished at death.

If death is the end of the coexistence between the fields of super-energy and the physical body, then what is the beginning? When do the higher energy bodies descend to enter into coincidence with a physical body?

There have been many arguments over when the soul joins the body.

According to some traditions, the soul enters the body at conception. Others say that the incarnating soul is free to join the body at any time between conception and a month or two after birth. Within this latter view, it is even argued that the soul may come and go during this period, thereby deferring the final decision whether to 'accept' the body or not. The distressing phenomenon of cot death, for which medical science has no explanation, is said by some to be the consequence of an early decision by the conscious incarnating soul to leave its new physical vehicle.

It may also be that the process of incarnation is progressive. If the human energy body is a composite of an ascending series of super-energy fields, not all of them need join the physical body at the same time. It may be that the lower fields, responsible for basic life functions, join the body first.

The higher fields may enter later. This idea might explain the relatively sudden advances in mental and other facilities seen in developing children. It also offers intriguing parallels with the sequence of initiation rites in some cultures, and, in the Christian tradition, sacraments, administered at key ages; perhaps they were originally designed to facilitate the integration of higher levels of function corresponding to the entrance of each higher level of super-energy 'body'.

Another perspective on progressive incarnation comes from the principle that in gestation, a human embryo passes through all the stages of evolution, from a single cell organism through a fish-like creature, to a primate with a tail and eventually to the full human form. It may be that at each stage, the level of super-energy corresponding to animals at that stage of evolution comes in to join the developing embryo. The highest bodies of super-energy may not be able to coexist with the physical body in its immature state, coming into incarnation only when the body reaches full adult maturity.

If the real essence of an individual is a subtle body of super-energy which incarnates into a physical body for a certain period of time, it is obvious that death could be followed by reincarnation into a new body.

Conception and death could be compared to stepping in and out of motor cars. The driver corresponds to the super-energy body and the motor car to the physical body. Super-energy animates the physical body just as the driver activates the car.

A new body would be a natural destination for a super-energy field which has just left an old one in the same way that a driver, having discarded a worn-out car, will sooner or later acquire another one – unless, of course, he has given up motoring or found a more advanced mode of transport!

In most ancient religions, reincarnation was accepted without question. Today there is renewed interest in this subject and a considerable amount of evidence has being collected to support it.

One of those to have conducted a painstaking scientific study of reincarnation is Dr Ian Stevenson of the University of Virginia. Dr Stevenson collected evidence from all over the world. Over a period of twenty years he considered 2,000 cases indicative of people having inhabited a human body prior to the one they occupy at present. Dr Stevenson published his findings in over twenty books and articles in journals from 1960 onwards. Stevenson admits that not even all the cases investigated together provide *proof* for reincarnation. They do however provide "a body of evidence, suggestive of reincarnation, that appears to be growing in amount and quality".

Dr Stevenson has concentrated his researches on what many regard as the most incontrovertible evidence for reincarnation, namely the testimony of young children. These are cases in which small children appear to have spontaneous recollections of a past life, frequently speaking and behaving as though they have just left another human body and revealing detailed memories of other times, people, and places. The following is typical of the many cases investigated and documented by Dr Stevenson.

The story concerns a boy born in France with a number of small birthmarks.

As soon as he could speak he indicated that these were marks left by bullets which had killed him. As his speech developed he named the men who had killed him, one of whom had accused him of cheating at cards. He identified members of his previous family, his girlfriend, and where he had lived – which turned out to be a village in Sri Lanka.

His French parents had great difficulty with him. He ate with his hands, rejecting the family food, demanding rice and curries and a drink called *arak*. He wanted to play cards and rather than western clothes he preferred to wrap a cloth about himself like a Ceylonese sarong. Frequently, he broke into a language his family couldn't understand, which turned out to be Sinhalese. He also climbed trees with amazing agility, saying that he was going after coconuts.

On investigation, it transpired that a coconut picker in Sri Lanka with the name given by the child had been murdered during a card game several years before the birth of the French boy. After the age of five, these strange memories of a life in Sri Lanka faded and the child grew up quite normally.

It is not uncommon for young children between the ages of two and four to speak as though they have had a previous existence either on earth or in some other dimension. Furthermore it is obvious to most parents that children have their own personality from the moment of birth. Unfortunately in the West the personality of infants and what they have to say is rarely taken seriously. By the time the children have sufficient vocabulary to express themselves fully, their memories of a previous existence have usually faded away.

One of over 1,000 cases investigated by another researcher in America, Hemendra Banerjee, concerned a three-year old girl in Des Moines, Iowa. The girl, Romy Crees, talked repeatedly of being a man called Joe Williams, with a wife named Sheila and three children. Romy said that she lived as Joe Williams in Charles City, about 140 miles away. She even described his mother – Louise – mentioning such details as a pain in her right leg and her favourite flowers.

Romy was eventually taken to Charles City, a Mrs Louise Williams was tracked down in the phone book, and the two met. Mrs Williams knew no one in Des Moines and was astonished at the information the little girl appeared to have. Nonetheless, she was able to confirm that Romy was correct in every detail. In the house, the little girl had even recognised a photograph of Sheila and the children taken with Joe. Joe had died in a road accident two years before Romy was born.

There does seem to be a pattern in these extraordinary cases. A violent death followed by a rapid reincarnation appears to leave the new child with a vivid recollection of the previous life. Perhaps a longer sojourn in the heavenly realms between incarnations, along with the experiences that go with it, push past-life memories into deeper recesses of the psyche.

Dr Karl Muller is another researcher into reincarnation who investigated cases in which children spontaneously recalled past lives. By coincidence one of his best cases also involved Sri Lanka.

In 1956, a girl called Gnanatilleka was born into a Tamil family at Hedunawa in Sri Lanka. At the age of two she claimed to have other parents.

She developed a phobia for elephants. At four she began to speak Sinhalese and recalled a former life in a village called Talawakelle, sixteen miles from her present home. She spoke of being a boy called Turin. She described her former parents, brothers and sisters. She also recalled a jewellery theft in the family, the way her father brushed his hair, her mother's stoutness and the need for her family to buy firewood because no coconut trees grew at Talawakelle. She also had a vivid recollection of an accident with an elephant in which she had died.

On investigation it transpired that fifteen months before the birth of Gnanatilleka a twelve year old boy called Turin had been killed by an elephant.

The details of his family corresponded to those described by Gnanatilleka and the girl recognised her former family with delight. The girl had a birthmark on her knee and suffered from abdominal pains which correlated with the location of the fatal injuries received by Turin in his accident.

Stevenson and Muller often found that birthmarks correlated with injuries sustained at death in a previous life.

Inexplicable phobias and pains have also been traced back to a traumatic death in a previous incarnation. In one case cited by Dr Muller, acute abdominal pains appeared to have a terrible origin in a previous life. In 1952, a man from Zurich was visiting a zoo. While watching a monkey in its cage, he was suddenly overcome by agonising stomach cramps. For five months, he suffered without relief. Eventually, his problem was diagnosed as psychosomatic and he was recommended to practise meditation. After a week of this practice, the patient had a vision involving sight, smell and sound. He became aware of himself tied to a stake on a platform in a medieval town. A dignitary from a church tribunal was reading an accusation, from which he later recalled only his name, Jan van Leyden. Then an executioner, dressed in a red cloak, came up and disembowelled him with red hot pincers. He lost consciousness and woke up to find himself in a mutilated state, suspended in a cage high above the town. In the cage he died an agonising death. Two other victims, who had suffered the same fate, died alongside him in separate cages.

Within four weeks of this dreadful vision the abdominal pain faded away.

The vision prompted him to undertake several weeks of research in libraries. Eventually he uncovered the story of a Jan van Leyden, executed in 1536 in precisely the barbaric manner he had relived in the vision. With the story was an illustration of three cages hanging from a church tower.

Whilst some children and adults occasionally have spontaneous recollections of a previous life, the great majority of information to support the idea of reincarnation comes from the use of a technique called hypnotic regression.

Many researchers have worked in the field of hypnotic regression since the subject first caught the public eye in the 1950s when Morey Bernstein published his famous book, *The Search for Bridey Murphy*. Bernstein used hypnotic regression to take a 29-year old American woman called Virginia Tighe into what appeared to be a previous incarnation. Under hypnosis, her accent changed and she became an 18th century Irish girl from Cork called Bridey Murphy.

The information given by Mrs Tighe under hypnosis was detailed and descriptive and appeared to be very authentic. Given that she had no detailed knowledge of Ireland in this life, nor had she visited the country prior to her regression, the accounts were difficult to explain in normal ways. They were taken by Bernstein to be the recall of a previous life – although it was difficult to verify the information completely as records in Ireland did not go back that far.

The volume of material now published on hypnotic regression into past lives is enormous. As with UFOs, a critic can find fault with individual accounts, but when the whole body of evidence is considered it is unreasonable to dismiss it all out of hand.

In addition to remembering what appears to be a past life on earth, some people have a memory of an existence in other realms between their lives on earth.

Another researcher into reincarnation, Dr Frederick Lenz, investigated fifteen cases of people who claimed to remember a period of existence in a non-physical world. These people recalled their death in a past life, a passage through other worlds after death, and subsequently their rebirth in the next incarnation. The early stages of these recollected journeys included many features of the near-death experience as documented by Dr Moody. In the later stages, people reported passing through a number of ascending regions or 'worlds', each one being quite different from the one before.

Dr Lenz found that the description of these worlds by his subjects bore a striking similarity to the accounts contained in the Tibetan Book of the Dead, of all the world's religious texts the most explicit in its description of after-death experiences. They also contain many elements which echo the teachings of other religious traditions including Christian ideas of heaven and hell. Referring to his experience in the first of these purported non-physical worlds, one man said,

> I found myself in a disgusting place. I was tormented by the people there. They were deformed and awful. They kept chasing me and asking me questions about my life. It was a nightmare . . .
>
> I cannot tell you how long I stayed there . . . There was no feeling of time passing.

Another reported,

> I felt like I was in a foreign country. I had a body but it was not physical, although it was the same shape as my physical body had been. I found myself in this bleak landscape, and near me there were two people fighting and arguing . . . although they kept hurting each other, it seemed as if they could not do any permanent damage to each other. The shrieks coming from them were so ungodly, so appalling, that my only thought was to get away from them . . . I was very unhappy in this world. When the time came for me to leave, I felt like I was being let out of prison. It was a great relief to leave that place behind.

As people moved on through each of the higher worlds, they reported that they felt as if they left behind a part of themselves that was no longer needed, as if he or she were shedding successive layers. From these reports it would seem that people pass through a series of lives after death. Just as the physical body is shed at death, so successive layers of the energy body would appear to be shed in each transition to higher realms of the universe.

People indicated that each world was somehow 'brighter' or 'higher' than the last. The second of these worlds was generally described as a more reflective place, a world of pure thought in which knowledge, ideas, symbols and images could be grasped and manipulated with great clarity and ease.

When they reached the third of these worlds, some of Dr Lenz' subjects felt that they achieved a proper understanding of themselves and of reality for the first time. One woman described the experience in the following terms,

> I felt that all my life I had been dressed in a costume but I didn't know it. One day the costume fell away and I saw what I really had been all along. I was not what I thought I was. All my life I had thought of myself as a person, as a body. I thought to myself, 'I am so and so, a woman, a mother, a secretary,' and things like that.
>
> When I went into this world I realised that all along I was not those things. I was a soul, not a body. I couldn't die; I couldn't be born. I lived forever. I wasn't a male or female. It was like waking up after having amnesia. I was overjoyed to be "me" again. I had been all along, but I had lost sight of it and thought that I was a physical body. My body was only a thing I used for my life on earth. When it wore out, I got rid of it.

In this world, some people reported being greeted by friends and relatives who had already died; even though they did not have physical bodies, they recognised them intuitively:

> I saw my wife, the soul that had been my wife. We had been together for many lives before. She greeted me. I felt such love for her, I felt her love for me. She was a globe of light. There were other globes there too, but I knew her right away from the others.
>
> She wasn't a 'she' like she had been on earth when I knew her. She didn't have a sex; neither did I.

Some people also recalled encountering 'angels' during their passage through this world:

> There was nothing but joy there, and colours – such beautiful colours. These were not like the colours on earth; they were deeper and richer. They had sounds and scents too . . . There were many types of beings there. Beautiful beings like angels. They came to me and helped me. They were so innocent and pure. They told me that I would soon be going to an even higher world where I would rest and that they were here to help me understand everything that was happening to me.

Finally, people reported reaching an ultimate resting place, where they seemed to stay for a very long time. A number of people described this world as composed of countless levels and subworlds, in which each person automatically gravitated to the most appropriate and comfortable level. One woman remembered it as follows:

> I found myself in a vast place. I felt as though I had come home. I had no apprehensions, fears or worries. I no longer remembered my former life on earth. Nothing existed for me but a quiet fulfilment. I was not conscious of time in the usual sense; everything seemed timeless. I felt as if I had always been there. It was similar to the feeling I have when I wake from a dream that has seemed very real, only to discover that it wasn't real but only a dream. That is how I felt. My former life on earth had been a passing dream which I had now awakened from.
>
> I did not have the sense that I was moving in space. Everything was consciousness and pure awareness; there were no dimensions there. I moved through thousands of levels. On each level different souls were resting before being born again. The lower levels were much darker. I somehow knew that the souls on these levels were not as mature as those on the higher levels. Finally I reached a level that I was comfortable on. I stayed there. I sensed that there were many levels above the one I stopped at and that souls that were more advanced than I would go there.

Just as there is variation in near-death experiences, so there is a variation in the experiences people have further away from the point of death. Just as on earth, not everyone seems to have the same experience, and even common elements may be described differently by different people.

Furthermore, people tend to give an account which is consistent with their religious and other beliefs. However, Dr Lenz observed that there was a remarkable degree of consistency, with people for the most part experiencing very similar phenomena in exactly the same sequence.

The fact that descriptions of out-of-body experience are sometimes culturally specific does not invalidate them. It seems only natural that people would interpret new experiences in terms of an existing mind-set, conditioned by their life on Earth. This happens all the time. For example, aborigines seeing TV or hearing radio for the first time have taken them to be 'spirit boxes', communicating with dead ancestors, and aircraft to be silver dragons in the sky. These people are not hallucinating, but are cloaking a real experience in a familiar garb.

The descriptions of non-physical worlds collected by Dr Lenz resemble those received through mediums and purported to come from the dead. In passing from one realm to the next, Dr Lenz' subjects describe 'shedding' a layer and leaving it behind. Spiritualists also speak of a number of ascending levels and of vehicles – such as the 'astral shell' – which are left behind in lower levels. Thus not only the evidence of the living but also that of the dead supports the idea that the universe consists of a number of distinct realms, arranged in an ascending sequence.

It is also possible to see close links between spiritualist beliefs and the cosmology presented earlier in this book. Spiritualists talk of a number of different levels or worlds, each having a higher 'rate of vibration' or frequency. We have postulated a series of realms, each formed out of a different, higher speed of primal movement. Spiritualists say that a spiritual being has to raise or lower its 'vibration rate' to move from one level to another. We have postulated that movement from one realm to another would be possible by raising or lowering the speed of energy. These descriptions are compatible; like the hum of a spinning top, the spin of energy in the vortex would increase in frequency as the energy within it moves faster.

To complete the chapter, we quote in full one of the most remarkable accounts collected by Dr Lenz which includes not only a vivid description of the experience of death but also of experiences in higher realms after death.

The story concerns a department store manager from Chicago who was on a camping trip with his family. One morning, he was watching the sun rise over the mountains when he had the following extraordinary recollection.

> I remembered a past life of mine in, what I would guess, judging from the style of dress and cars, was around the 1930s. In that life I owned a small business in a small mid-western town.
>
> I was walking quickly along the sidewalk when I felt a stabbing pain in my chest. My whole body reeled and I felt incredibly dizzy. I tried to steady myself, but I was seized by a wave of nausea. I reached out to try to support myself and found myself falling towards the ground.
>
> The pain got much worse. I closed my eyes and felt myself gasping for breath. My heart was pounding so loudly that I couldn't even think.
>
> I opened my eyes for a moment and saw that a crowd of faces was gathered above me. A man I had seen working in my building was reaching down and loosening my necktie. One woman was telling someone to go get an ambulance. It was then that I realised that I had had a heart attack.
>
> Another wave of pain shot through me, much worse than the first.
>
> Everything around me grew hazy; then I felt my whole body spasm and shudder. A series of pictures from my childhood appeared before me. They were followed by scenes from my youth and then scenes from my adult life.
>
> I saw the most important stages of my life passing before my eyes in seconds. Then I was swallowed up by blackness and lost consciousness.
>
> I have no idea how long I was unconscious. I was in unfamiliar surroundings in a room somewhere. Everything appeared to be very misty and hazy. I could see some people in the room, furniture, curtains. I could even hear them talking. But they seemed like phantoms to me; they didn't seem solid. I walked over to them and asked them who they were and where I was. They ignored me. I repeated my request. They seemed very agitated by something; the woman was crying and those around her were trying to comfort her. I became very impatient because they were ignoring me, and I moved closer to them. It was then that I began to suspect that something was wrong with me. I noticed that I didn't exactly walk over to them but sort of glided next to them without having to physically move. I peered at the woman who was crying and at those around

her. They seemed very familiar to me. I felt that I had known them at some earlier time in my life. With shock I recognised that the 'woman' was my wife. She was surrounded by my two sons and several of my relatives. I called them by name and asked them what was wrong. Still they didn't seem to hear me. I was in a quandary as to what to do. Then I remembered going to work that morning and having a heart attack. A funny thought entered into me. "I'm dead", I thought. "Well, now what am I supposed to do?". Then I was filled with a feeling of self-pity. I thought, "Oh God, I don't want to be dead. Everyone I love is here and they can't even see me". I felt miserable and watched them helplessly.

For a time I watched the people in the room. They were putting on their coats and hats. Their movements seemed very mechanical, as if they were robots or humanoids. I felt alienated from them. I felt the urge to go with them. An outside force was compelling me, pulling me to go. I found myself outside my house beside my car. I saw my brother-in-law driving it. This made me mad. I started to tell him not to drive my car when I realised again that I was dead. It really didn't matter whether he drove it or not.

Then I felt myself moving forward again. I saw that I could move anywhere I wanted to at will. I just wished where I wanted to be, and I was there almost at once. I wished to go with my family, and the next thing I knew I was in a room crowded with people. I found I didn't have to work my way around the crowd but could actually walk through the people there.

Everyone's attention was directed to the front of the room. I saw with some surprise that my body was lying there in a coffin. I was seized with an immediate feeling that I wanted to get back into my body and be alive again.

But at the same instant I also knew that this was impossible; my body was dead, and it would never be alive again. All I could do was wait and watch. I saw all of the people I had known come and see me. I saw my family, friends, even the priest from my church. I was very interested to see how upset many of them were. I could see that some people were very disturbed and cried a great deal. Others had just come because it was expected of them. This angered me. I saw the expression of each one.

Then I felt the force moving me again. I had seen enough; I wanted to leave.

I cannot tell you how long I stayed on earth because I

I cannot tell you how long I stayed on earth because I had no real conception of time. I wandered from place to place, visiting all the familiar places I had been during my life. I went to my mother's old house, my old high school and many other places. Finally I sensed that I had to leave the earth. I didn't belong there anymore . . .

I found myself in another world. There were terrible sounds all around me. I could hear a constant thundering and whistling, also loud booms and non-human cries. The place I was in was filled with broken things, twisted wreckage like a scrap heap. The air was filled with hazy smoke. There were lots of different beings all around me. Many of them were fighting each other. Their howls and cries were so loud that I wanted to run away. I roamed in this world for a long, long time.

Occasionally I would see other people like myself. I felt like a stranger in a strange land. Several times the beings there – awful-looking things that were like deformed people – tried to bother me. I found that if I ignored them, they would go away.

Then I left that world and found myself in a realm of ideas. This was a nicer world than the other one. It was filled with voices, singing, music, things like that. I was different in this world myself. That is, when I was in the twisted world my body had been similar to the one I had used on earth after my death. But that body had left me when I came into this world. Now I was not physical; I wasn't shaped like I had been, with hands and arms. I was lighter and clearer. It was more like I was an essence . . . I stayed in this world and then passed to an even more beautiful one filled with many different-coloured lights. They were beautiful. I could hear a kind of music all the time. But it wasn't music in the way that we normally think of music. All of existence was in kind of harmony. Life itself was music. My being was different in this world too – it was lighter and more luminous. I liked it here very much.

It was in this world that I saw people I knew who had died before me. My father and several others I had known came. They greeted me. They did not look like they had on earth. They were luminous beings. But I knew who they were. They welcomed me with great joy.

Then I passed into an even 'higher' world. It had millions of levels. I could see levels below me, but not really above me. The light there was dazzling. I could see that the beings on the levels below me were not as aware as I was. I rested here; I knew it was a place of rest.

I was infused with a golden light.

The rest seems so remote now. When I saw all this it was clearer, but even then I couldn't have described it. There aren't any words for it. It is being with God; that's the best way I can describe it.

CHAPTER 13

God and the Gods

Man has always questioned his existence. Is there a purpose and destiny to human life? If there really is a continuity of existence before birth and after death, what is the point of our lives on this planet? If, as people report, we feel more at home in higher realms of the universe, why are we here at all? What are we supposed to be doing? Is it all just a game? Are we meant to just enjoy ourselves, or suffer, depending upon our luck? Or is there some vital significance to our lives here on Earth? If there is a deeper purpose, what is it? And who or what set up the whole business in the first place?

Throughout history, man has sought answers to these ultimate questions in the idea of the gods. More recently, religions have taught people to believe in a single God. But how relevant are these ideas of God and the gods today? Is there really a creator of the universe, or is the idea of God dead, as modern science would have us believe?

In classical science, the existence of God was accepted without question. God was thought to have created matter and originated all the laws governing its behaviour. Classical scientists, such as Sir Isaac Newton, believed that they were merely uncovering the laws that God had established.

With the advance of science, however, not only the role, but the very existence of God came into question. In the 19th century, Darwin's theory of evolution challenged the idea of God as creator, explaining the origin and diversity of life as a natural rather than a supernatural process. Man came to be seen as an accident of evolution. In the 20th century, physics has come to view the unfolding universe as self-creating from its beginning in a *Big Bang*. In this scheme of things there is really no place at all for God.

Modern science has decided that there is no need for a creator of the universe. However with the vortex, everything changes. The concept of a creator becomes absolutely vital.

The universe seems to exist in its own right. It gives the impression of being completely independent and self-sustaining. However the vortex challenges this common sense notion.

The vortex totally undermines the concept of material substance existing as an independent reality. It shows how everything – including matter, space and time – is a form of energy. But what is energy if not pure movement?

In this new scheme of things, it is movement and not material that is the reality underlying the universe. There is nothing concrete in the universe whatsoever. There is no underlying material there at all. Movement is the sole reality.

This is a staggering thought. People mostly imagine our world to be made up of substantial things that move. In reality, it is quite the opposite.

Movement exists first and foremost. Everything in the physical universe is relative to the speed of light, which is itself a measure of movement. Pure movement creates our world – from light and warmth to the wind and rain, from trees and mountains to the laughter of children playing.

But what can this movement be? How can there be movement if there is nothing to move? In this *primordial* movement, there is nothing concrete at all. It is movement without any substance in it. This movement seems to be an abstraction. Could it be that the movement underpinning the universe is an abstract reality? Could it be purely the idea of movement? Is the universe but a *vision* of movement, a pure act of imagination?

If the movement underlying energy is an act of pure imagination, then every particle of matter is simply *imagined* into existence. Every bit of energy and super-energy is nothing but an idea.

Having excluded the concept of material, we are led to the conclusion that the entire universe is an immense, unfolding vision. In the words of Michael Faraday, *"All this is a dream"*. The entire universe is nothing but a dream.

There cannot be a dream without a dreamer. There cannot be an act of imagination without one that imagines. If the universe, from minute atom to mighty galaxy, is an unfolding vision then there must be someone behind it.

There must be some One responsible for this immense act of creative imagination. This, man calls God. As the modern teacher Maharaji has said, *"This world that we see is the imagination of God"*.

A dream is inextricably bound to its dreamer; it is the act of the dreamer. Should the dreamer cease to dream, the dream vanishes as though it had never existed. Were the universal act of imagination to cease, then the entire universe would disappear without trace. Every particle of matter, even space itself, would vanish in an instant. They are totally dependent upon the continuous act of creation. This would explain the ancient teaching that God created the universe out of nothing and that, without God, the universe could not be.

Matter and light have no independent reality. As acts of imagination, they are utterly dependent on that which imagines, as a dream is utterly dependent on the dreamer. Creation was not a one-off event. The universe is in a continual state of creation. Each and every bit of energy in the universe, every particle of matter in our world, is an act of *continuing* creative imagination. Each vortex is continuously being imagined into existence; it is part of an ongoing dream.

When one considers the immensity of the universe, the scope of this act of imagination is bewildering. There are thousands of particles in each human blood cell. Yet a blood cell is almost nothing; five million would fit in a pin-head. So how many particles must there be in just one human body? There are litres of blood in the body, and bone and tissue besides. Then there are five billion bodies. But what is the whole mass of humanity compared to the planet itself? Yet the Earth itself is merely a speck of matter orbiting a small star; there are billions of other stars in our galaxy and galaxies themselves are beyond count to modern astronomy. So how many particles must there be in the entire physical realm of the universe? Each is an individual act of imagination. But even the entire realm of matter and light is only a small part of the total universe. Science has found no end to the physical universe and hasn't even begun to probe the super-physical realms. The power of the creative principle behind the universe defies comprehension. Being the source of everything it could be described as almighty.

Equally staggering is the immense duration of this focused act of attention. Consider the life-span of each particle in an atom. The proton has a life expectancy estimated at a billion, trillion, trillion, trillion years. That is a long time for a continual act of uninterrupted concentration.

Is it meaningful to look for an original moment of creation in a far and distant time? The universe exists through the imagining of forms of energy. Should the pattern of imagination be changed, so would these forms. All forms in the universe could instantly alter with a change in the pattern of universal imagination. Even though each particle vortex exists now, it could conceivably vanish in a moment. It could have come into existence a moment ago.

By imagining movement, the creator brings into being the manifold forms of the universe and the dimensions which separate them, such as space and time. Space and time do not exist independently of the universe, because they are created by movement. There is no possibility of space-time separation between the creator and the universe. The creator is neither inside nor outside time.

The universal dreamer and the dream are inextricably bound together in the absolute here and now, the eternal present. God could only pre-exist the universe, and continue after its demise, if time existed beyond the universe. Past and future, along with all other forms of separation, are mere facets of the dream. There can be no separation in God whatsoever; within God, there can be no distinctions of any kind.

A human dreamer can live apart from his dream; the dreamer alone is real and the dream is as nothing. This analogy suggests that the creator alone is real and vital to the creation. Without the dreamer, the universal dream could not exist. But could the universal dreamer exist without the dream? Could the creator exist without the creation? If God were defined solely as the creator of the universe, then the answer would have to be no. If the universal dreamer were to stop dreaming, it would cease to be a dreamer and so cease to be.

A dream is distinct from the dreamer. Likewise the creation is quite distinct from the creator. This account of the universe is not a form of pantheism. Pantheism claims that God is the substance of everything, that all things are formed out of God. The universe is formed out of movement which has no substance, be it material or God. Movement is the act of God, not the substance of God.

So what is the creator? What is God?

To begin with, consider the universe. If the universe is an unfolding act of imagination, it could be viewed as a vast body of thought. Every movement, every bit of energy, would be a thought-form. Every particle of matter and light, as an act of imagination, would be a thought in the mind of God. Could it be that the universe in its entirety is simply the mind of God?

In mind, we see the conjunction of consciousness and thought. Mind could also be regarded as the body of thought. But consciousness is quite distinct from thought. Consciousness is not thought, it is the awareness that lies behind thought. Consciousness can exist without thought, but without consciousness there is no awareness of thought.

Perhaps there are only two fundamental realities, consciousness and thought. If the universe is the mind of God, then God would be the consciousness underlying it.

The two realities could also be described as consciousness and energy. Consciousness is the creative principle, and energy the universe it creates.

Consciousness is not energy, nor is it the consequence of any form of energy. Rather, consciousness is the source of all energy, pervading the whole of creation even to the sub-atomic level. Consciousness is present in everything. Like the eye in a hurricane, consciousness would be present even in the vortex of energy, right at the heart of the atom. Consciousness is the prime reality, the ground of all existence.

Consciousness could be taken to correspond to 'spirit'. In the past, the word spirit has been used very loosely to describe anything intangible. But if spirit is defined as consciousness, then it could be said that 'spirit' is within everything, from the greatest of beings to the lowliest particles of matter. However, only the one God would be pure spirit. Everything else in existence would be a form of energy through which the spirit is made manifest.

The creator of the universe is the unseen consciousness in all things. It experiences everything but judges nothing. It is the source of all power, yet remains untouched by power. It is all-seeing and yet unseen. Simultaneously totally imminent and totally transcendent, it is the all-knowing experience of everything that exists. It is as if God creates the universe and then experiences through every single part of it. God experiences being a blade of grass and a tree, being an eagle and a dolphin, being you and being me.

Consciousness is the most obvious attribute of the creator. However the creation of the universe also involves will, love, and intelligence. These must also be attributes of the creator. The creation is an act of conscious imagination, shaped by intelligence, activated by love, and impelled by will. This is what the creator puts in; experience is what the creator receives back.

These diverse attributes need not imply separation in the creator. They could correspond to the different facets of the creator. Just as we experience matter, space and time as separate aspects of the one, undivided vortex of energy, so we would experience the creator simultaneously as consciousness and will, intelligence and love.

Through understanding consciousness, we can begin to appreciate who we really are. If consciousness is the ground of all existence, there can be no separation in consciousness; consciousness must be single and undivided. This conclusion is also bornc out by physics.

In our common experience, no two things are identical. No two snowflakes, flowers or persons are precisely the same. However, at a sub-atomic level, this is not the case. The most basic forms of matter are the elementary particles. Yet, within each type, all particles appear to be the same. For example, all protons throughout the universe seem to have identical physical characteristics. This uniformity of elementary particles strongly suggests that a single consciousness underlies them all; that they are all, so to speak, shaped by a single hand. If protons were being created by separate sparks of consciousness, it seems likely that they would differ from one another in their characteristics.

If consciousness is indivisible, then consciousness cannot be separate in each individual. Different life forms manifest different levels of consciousness, according to their degree of development. But we are all one in our essential being. We are all the same consciousness aware of the world through different bodies, looking out of many different eyes, cut off from one another only by an illusion of separation.

The consciousness aware of your thoughts and feelings, behind the seeing of your eyes and the hearing of your ears, is the same consciousness within me.

This is what the indivisibility of consciousness really means. Behind our many thoughts and feelings, within our different bodies, we are all one. We see our physical bodies as being separate from each other and in our private thoughts and feelings we experience further separation. However, in consciousness there is no separation; our underlying consciousness is the same universal, undivided principle that manifests through everyone and everything. If this is God, then, in our essential being, each and every one of us is God.

In his essence man is one with God whether he believes it or not. God is not separate from man, for God is at the heart of man's very consciousness – not his thoughts and emotions, but the pure awareness behind them. God is the seat of man's being, the well-spring of his love, intelligence and will. For man to search for God outside of himself is pointless because God lies within him. We are already united with God whether we know it or not. All we have to do is wake up and realise it.

But is this awakening the whole aim and purpose of human life? If we are already in essence God, what is there left to achieve?

One clue to understanding the purpose of human life is to realise that God, as pure consciousness, has no form and can manifest only through forms. Consciousness is present in every aspect of creation to some degree. It is the essence of being human to recognise consciousness within ourselves. It could be that, as human beings, we have the unique opportunity to expand into full consciousness of our divine nature and become an expression of God on Earth.

In doing so, we become a god.

A clear distinction needs to be made between God and the gods. God is the consciousness which creates the universe as an unfolding act of imagination. God is not a person or being, rather God is the animator of all persons and beings.

The gods are entirely different from God. The gods are highly evolved beings that manifest the attributes and powers of God. However, the gods are still part of creation; as forms of energy, they exist within the universe only as part of the universal dream.

Planets such as the Earth could be training centres for the gods. Life on Earth could be our opportunity to become a god; it could be viewed as a workshop for our personal development as gods. This idea is embodied in the word 'human' which means 'god-man'. We all have the potential to become gods. Jesus Christ, for example, fulfilled this potential to become a full manifestation of God on Earth. As for the rest of us, we are gods in the making.

Becoming a god and manifesting divine powers is not a question of gaining anything. It is just a matter of uncovering our true nature. The powers of the gods are latent within us all. They are part of our evolutionary path.

Numerous saints and mystics have these powers, which in India are called siddhis. These seemingly miraculous powers are simply the power of God manifesting through them. Many powers, such as clairvoyance, simply reflect the consciousness which is the ground of our being. Others, including bilocation and materialisation, involve the transubstantiation of matter, that is, acceleration through the light-barrier. But this is also a reflection of universal consciousness. It is universal consciousness which imagines the underlying movement – that is, energy – in the first instance. Therefore it is consciousness alone which can accelerate this movement. It is only consciousness that can change the substance of energy. From this standpoint, it is clear that the mastery of divine powers can only come with greater consciousness. The obvious way to attain them is, not through the growth of a new technology, but through a growth in consciousness.

There is a lot of unfounded fear surrounding supernatural powers. The powers of the gods are generally attained as a consequence of personal growth and development. They usually unfold as spontaneous gifts. A person may work over many years, maybe even lifetimes, striving to grow in consciousness. Then suddenly strange powers appear quite unexpectedly.

Most saints and mystics attach little importance to these

powers, seeing them as incidental in the approach to God. At the other end of the spectrum, there are those who seek the power of the gods as an end in itself. What really matters, however, is not how the powers are attained, but the use a person makes of them.

Some people exploit them – perhaps unwittingly – in the service of their own egos. Needing attention, and wanting to control those they help, they dominate through fear and manipulate through flattery. It is not for us to judge other people's lives – we each have our path of evolution. But for our own protection, it is important to discern where someone is coming from. There is a glamour surrounding the psychic which makes it easy for people to deceive both themselves and others. Highly gifted individuals can attract large followings, and even come to be regarded as divine. However, it is not a person's claims or the powers they display that are important; it is not their signs or wonders, but their personal quality that counts. The question is, who are they serving, themselves or others? Sometimes it is hard to tell. The ability to discern requires experience and insight. There is a tendency in us all to be driven compulsively by personal desires and unmet emotional needs. We all have to meet our own needs, and serve ourselves as well as others. What counts is the balance we achieve between these two aspects.

The root of the problem is all too often the pursuit of power. Not satisfied with what they can achieve on their own account, some people seek to augment their power with supernatural forces. They seek an ally on the 'other side'. Such people tend to draw to themselves entities who in their turn are seeking power in the physical plane, through the intermediary of a human being. To begin with the human being may believe that he is the master, but he can very quickly end up as the servant.

The problem is that it is often unclear what type of entity we are dealing with. Whilst most supernatural entities are benign, others are definitely not. The more we are in harmony within ourselves, and the greater our integrity, the more we live with love and a good sense of humour, the less likely are we to attract malign entities. It is through fear and taking ourselves too seriously that we lay ourselves open to their influence.

There is nothing wrong with working in conjunction with the supernatural. We are all assisted in this way much of the time, usually without realising it. The ability to channel information and harness power from intelligent entities in higher realms is an important gift which gives people such as healers and psychics an opportunity to help others. But there are dangers in this area. We may, for example, mistake their communication or misunderstand it; this happens on Earth all the time, even when we have all the evidence of the senses to help us.

Furthermore, it is easy to credit supernatural beings with all sorts of qualities they may not have. It would be absurd to suppose that all discarnate beings are infinitely knowledgeable, wise and loving. Nonetheless, many people believe that if they get a message from 'upstairs' it must be right. But these beings without bodies – like us beings with bodies – are not infallible. For instance, they mostly appear to have very little grasp of terrestrial time.

There is a part of us that looks for parenting and the comfort of being told what to do. But we are not here as the blind instrument of higher external powers, like foot-soldiers who follow orders. We are here to learn to attune to our own divinity within. We should act in cooperation with others, both incarnate and discarnate, only in the fullness of our own wisdom.

To learn, we must be free to make mistakes. A child learning to stand or walk will fall over repeatedly before succeeding. The parents can only observe, and perhaps encourage. Supernatural beings would appear to treat us in much the same way. It would seem that they mainly stay deliberately behind the scenes. All the signs are that they respect the sacredness of our learning space. It is only when we get so out of hand that we are in danger of blowing up the school that they are likely to intervene.

If life on Earth is viewed as an opportunity for growth in godhood, the human situation could be likened to one of children at school and the planet Earth to a school for infant gods. In our development as gods, we would be continually learning lessons through our many experiences. As in any school, the majority would be students and the minority teachers who have volunteered to help the pupils in their learning.

We all need teachers to remind us of our true destiny. We are born into a state of forgetfulness, with no memory of who we really are or what we can become. In too secure and comfortable a situation, we are in danger of remaining unaware of the real meaning of our lives. We are liable to become small-minded and preoccupied with trivialities. To achieve the purpose of our lives, we need to wake up to our real potential; in this respect, disaster and suffering, illness and adversity can sometimes be a deliverance if they shake us out of sleep. Each change, in fact everything that happens in our life, can be taken as a learning experience. The role of the teacher is to help us as we learn from our experiences and, directing our attention to our inner reality, awaken within us our latent godhood.

Good teachers will encourage us to accept the totality of human experience. They help us to open up to our full potential – physical, mental, emotional, spiritual. In doing so, they can help us to find the only freedom that really matters, the freedom to be who we really are.

It is not that we cannot learn without teachers. But usually we can make far more rapid progress with a teacher than struggling away on our own. Lessons may take many years to grasp through personal experience unaided. Teachers, however, can give us direction to learn from our experience more quickly. They point out to us what is really going on – whether we are learning tennis or the skills of life.

To benefit from a teacher, there has to be a ripeness on the part of the student. Often, it is suffering or a crisis which brings us to this point of receptivity. Before then, teaching is liable to fall upon deaf ears. We can be told something, but it never seems to sink in. But when the pupil is ready, the teacher mysteriously appears. The teacher is always there, but we are unlikely to recognise him or her until we are ripe.

We benefit greatly if we can embrace more than one teaching. Some people become devoted to a particular teacher or teaching and find it hard to entertain the possibility that anyone else could be right. It can take courage to move from one teacher to another. But in the combination of different approaches we may find the particular balance that we need. Each of us is, after all, unique and we have to find our own individual path of evolution.

This is not to encourage the butterflies, that is, those who flit from teacher to teacher without really applying anything that they are taught. But attachment to a single teacher or teaching can be very limiting. We are multi-faceted, multi-levelled beings and few teachers are skilled in everything we need to learn. As we progress in the course of our lives, at each stage new challenges confront us, and our needs continually change as we grow.

To become a god, we need to recognise the enormous power of thoughts and emotions. Thought creates reality. To change our reality, we need to change our pattern of thinking, conscious and unconscious, and release the blocks on our emotions. Thoughts and emotions feed off each other. By choosing to replace negative thoughts with positive ones, by choosing not to feed negative emotions, and by freeing blocked emotional energy, we transform ourselves and the nature and quality of our experience.

Thoughts are real entities – they are as real as matter. Consciousness empowers thoughts. They depend upon consciousness for their very existence. Thoughts thrive on attention. As we entertain them, they grow and multiply. Before long we are totally lost in a whole train of thought.

Where to place our attention is ultimately the only freedom we have. Most of us are slaves to the thoughts which occupy our minds. There is a need to discriminate, to be master of our thoughts, choosing which to attend to and which to ignore. Instead, we get lost in imagination, identifying with our fears and desires. To use imagination properly is one of the greatest challenges facing us, and an essential step in becoming a god.

To become at one with God is another matter altogether. To experience the underlying unity of consciousness, we need to stop the mental chatter altogether. Normally we are conscious of things, of thoughts and emotions. Thus we are always caught up in the creation. Constantly searching for something to make our life complete, we experience duality and separation. Simply to be conscious, rather than to be conscious of anything, that is an objective in itself. Transcending all separation, we experience our unity with everything. Stepping out of duality, we experience ultimate peace.

In the East, many saints and mystics seem to emphasise the attainment of oneness with God while disparaging involvement with the world. In the West, on the contrary, most people overlook their need to achieve oneness with God, so involved are they with the world and creative activity. It could be that the fulfilment of our potential comes from bringing together the East and the West, from combining full Self-realisation with mastery of the god-like powers of creation.

If this is so, we need to develop ourselves at every level of our being. As we grow in awareness, we first discover the fragmentation of our being, and then realise the need to integrate body, mind and emotions into a balanced and harmonious whole. The older spiritual traditions disparaged the body and regarded all its desires as obstacles to be overcome. However, in reality, being in a human body is an unparalleled opportunity to have many and diverse learning experiences. Spirituality is not about escaping the body and its functions; it is about embracing our total reality. To come into balance, we need to integrate the primal aspects of our nature, not reject them. To become gods, we need to know ourselves fully in body, mind and emotions, and rediscover ourselves in spirit. Our opportunity is to realise not only our oneness with God, but also our full creative potential as human.

For we gods in the making, life on Earth is an unparalleled opportunity to learn the skills of creation in a domain where imagination can be exercised with comparative safety. For God, every act of imagination immediately becomes a reality in the universe. Even the realm of super-energy is far more plastic to thought than our world of matter. In the higher realms, imagination works instantly; the way things are imagined is exactly how they turn out to be. In these domains, mind and imagination have a terrific impact.

On Earth, the situation is quite different. Here, the fruits of thought and imagination manifest more slowly. We therefore have the opportunity to see and understand their effects. Matter provides the clay which enables us to explore our God-like powers of creation with relative safety. This is what makes the physical realm so suitable as a school for gods.

The freedom to experiment and make mistakes is essential to this learning process. Earth is an adventure playground where we can't really hurt ourselves, since even physical death cannot harm us. To play it safe, that is, not to take full advantage of our learning opportunities, is to miss the whole point of human life. The greatest risk in life is to risk nothing.

With freedom comes choice. We have the freedom either to pursue our own imaginings, or to align ourself with the unfolding act of universal imagination. We have a choice; it is all a question of where we place our attention. We can remain limited, attached to our own partial understandings and preoccupations, or attune ourselves to a more universal reality.

Consciousness never judges. There is no punishment meted out to those who follow their own imaginings to go their own way. Rather they experience separation and the fullness of their own fantasies, fears and imaginings.

Likewise there is no reward for those who choose to attune themselves to universal consciousness. For them rather, there is the experience of unity and the joy of fully expanded consciousness.

As we grow, we move on from seeking to achieve things purely for ourselves. We find ourselves as part of an unfolding pattern which is much bigger than our personal desires and ambitions. It is not that we miss out on personal fulfilment, but that what we want is in alignment with others. A single cell organism is very limited in its possibilities. But just as a single cell finds that it has all it requires and more when part of a multicellular organism, so we can achieve far more working in cooperation with others than struggling on our own.

In the past, religions taught that life on Earth was a period of trial, in which good behaviour would be rewarded by an eternity in heaven. They taught that happiness is not for this life in the body, but for the life hereafter.

But if we are in essence God, then the point is that we are free, really free, with the whole universe as our playground. Earth is not just a training ground for some life hereafter; it is an integral part of our eternal existence. The universe is ours, to do in as we want. The universe is not static. It is not a succession of obstacle courses to be negotiated, with our reward an eternity of rest in some heavenly realm. The universe is our play. It is our creation, because ultimately we ourselves are God. In the universe, we are constantly setting ourselves new challenges, devising new games, and having more and more outrageous adventures.

Some of us long to get out of the body and into the higher realms. We feel that life is like a maze. We are in it and we want to get out. To begin with we are confused. We try one way and another, but are foiled at every turn. We feel angry and frustrated, but gradually we begin to discover a pattern. Someone may help us so we begin to make progress. We remain convinced that our whole purpose is to get out of the maze and go home. But we chose to enter the maze in the first place. The experience of passing through it is what the game is all about. Every experience we have, good and bad, is all part of the play.

From this point of view, human life is just another game we have chosen to play. Will we remember who we are? Or, plunging into matter, will we lose ourselves in our creation? Will we recognise the incredible intricacy and perfection of the physical world as our own handiwork? Or will we spend lifetimes puzzling over who put it together, and why? How long will it take us to find our way out of the maze we have designed? And when we do, will we choose to stay, and revel in its possibilities? Or will we be hungry for new adventures elsewhere? Perhaps we will choose to set up new worlds, with even more intricate and difficult mazes, in which finding ourselves is even more challenging.

For the fun is in the journey, not the goal. The process of growth is such pleasure. The delight is in the rediscovery. There is such a joy in finding out again who we really are.

It is not that we are here to be servants of God, but to be fully God on Earth – that is our opportunity. If God is our own being, we serve God best by being fully ourselves. Our purpose is simply to act out and experience our real nature.

As far as consciousness is concerned, it doesn't really matter what we do. It is only the experience that counts. Like children at play, we can dress up and dance at different times in totally different ways. Morality and judgement don't come into it. Good and evil are just masks. It is all a game in the eternal play of creation. What we do and whether we have a good or bad time are a matter of sublime indifference.

But the creator is also love. It is complete and unconditional love that gives meaningful direction to the creation. With love come compassion and respect for the sacredness of all other beings.

Beings without love can grow in consciousness, will and intelligence, but ultimately they become parasites. Devoid of love themselves, they seek the adulation of others. In biological life, most parasites are organisms that were early experimental trials in the process of evolution. These models have some deficiency that makes it difficult for them to survive on their own. Instead, they latch on to a host for their nourishment.

In the early stages of the universe, supernatural beings are said to have developed embodying will, intelligence and consciousness, but not specifically love. It appears that we are part of a later experiment. We have the potential to evolve into a more complete image of God, being an embodiment of love as well as intelligence, will and consciousness. However, we can come under the influence of parasitic supernatural entities that seek to prey on us. They latch on to us through our fears and feed off our attention.

The most important thing for us is to learn to love. We can choose love rather than fear. We can experience the delight of growth and fulfilment, or the misery of stagnation. We can step out of our limitations, and live up to our full potential. Or we can stay stuck and live as less than we really are.

The choice is entirely ours: to express our innate magnificence, or to stay small; to acknowledge the enormous power within us, or to continue to pretend that we are helpless; to be mere mortals, or to live as gods.

Our mission on Earth is to become who we really are. To come into godhood, we don't have to forsake the world, or deny ourselves the enjoyment of it. Rather we need to grow both in consciousness and creativity. We need to develop our being as well as our doing. We require inner knowledge as well as worldly knowing. We need to achieve a state of balance in which we can enjoy earthly pleasures and the physical body – but at the same time pursue the unique opportunity presented by human life: to realise and demonstrate who we really are. Only in this balance can we enjoy life to the full and complete the divine purpose for which it is intended.

Bibliography

Banerjee, H.N. *Americans Who Have Been Reincarnated*; Macmillan, New York, 1980

Beard, Paul *Living On*, George Allen & Unwin, 1980

Bernstein, Morey *The Search for Bridey Murphy*, Pocket Books, New York, 1978

Burr, Harold Saxton *Blueprint for Immortality – The Electric Patterns of Life*, Neville Spearman, 1972

Buttlar, Johannes von *The UFO Phenomenon*, Sidgwick and Jackson, 1979

Cantor, G. N. and Hodge, M. J. S. *Conceptions of Ether: Studies in the History of Ether Theories*, Cambridge Univ Press 1981.

Clerk-Maxwell, James *Scientific Papers*, vol ii, 1890, pp 445-84

Christie-Murray, David *Reincarnation: Ancient Beliefs and Modern Evidence*, David & Charles, Newton Abbott, 1981

Dale, John *The Prince and the Paranormal: The Psychic Bloodline of the Royal Family*, W.H.Allen, London, 1986, (reporting text of British Medical Association press release, September 12, 1984)

Daniken, Eric von *Chariots of the Gods*, Corgi, 1972

Darwin, Charles *The Origin of Species*, 1859. Reprinted. London: Penguin

Dawkins, Richard *The Blind Watchmaker*, Penguin, 1988

Findhorn Community *The Findhorn Garden*, Turnstone Books/ Wildwood House, London 1976; Harper & Row, New York

Fisher, Joe *The Case for Reincarnation*, Granada, London 1985

Good, Timothy *Above Top Secret: The Worldwide UFO Cover-up* Sidgwick & Jackson, 1988

Green, Julian *Padre Pio's Multiple Miracles*, in *Miracles*, ed Martin Ebon, Signet, 1981

Hoyle, Sir Fred *The Intelligent Universe*, Michael Joseph, 1983

Huxley, Aldous *The Doors of Perception*, Penguin Books, 1959

Erlandur Haraldsson *Miracles are My Visiting Cards: An Investigative Report on the Psychic Phenomena Associated with Sathya Sai Baba*, Century Hutchinson, 1987

Erlandur Haraldsson & Karlis Osis *Appearance and Disappearance of objects in the presence of Sri Sathya Sai Baba*, Journal of the American Society for Psychical Research, Jan 1977

Helmholtz, Hermann *Ueber Integrale der hydrodynamischen Gleichungen, welche den Wirbelbewegungen entsprechen*, Crelle, 1858, (translated by Tait in *Phil. Mag.*, 1867)

Lenz, Frederick *Lifetimes*, The Bobbs-Merrill Company, New York, 1979
Lorimer, David *Survival? Body, Mind and Death in the Light of Psychic Experience*, Routledge & Kegan Paul, 1984
McCormmach, Russell, ed. *Historical Studies in the Physical Sciences*, Univ of Pennsylvania Press, Philadelphia 1970.
Monod, Jacques *Chance and Necessity*, Fontana, 1972
Moody, Raymond *Life after Life*, Bantam Books, 1976
Moreau, Francis *Visions and Prophecies of the Lady of Peace*, Wessex Research Group Newsletter No.14, Sherborne, 1988
Ramacharaka, Yogi *Advanced Course in Yogi Philosophy*, Fowler, 1904
Ravenscroft, Trevor *The Spear of Destiny*, Samuel Weiser, Maine, 1982
Ring, Kenneth *Life At Death*, Coward, McCann, and Geoghegan, New York, 1980
Sagan, Carl *The Cosmic Connection*, Coronet Books, 1973
Sheldrake, Rupert *A New Science of Life*, Paladin Books, 1987
Silliman, Robert H, *William Thomson: Smoke Rings and Nineteenth Century Atomism*, ISIS, Vol 54 (1963), pp 461-474.
Stanford, Ray *Fatima Prophecy: Days of Darkness, Promise of Light*, Association for the Understanding of Man, Austin, Texas
Stevenson, Dr Ian *Cases of the Reincarnation Type* vols 1-3, University of Virginia Press, Charlottesville
Stevenson, Dr Ian *Twenty Cases Suggestive of Reincarnation*, University of Virginia Press, Charlottesville, 1974
Thompson, S. P. *Life of William Thomson, Baron Kelvin of Largs*, London, 1910.
Thomson, J J. *Treatise on the Motion of Vortex Rings*, 1884
Thomson, William *Mathematical and Physical Papers 1841-1882*, 6 vols
Thomson, William *Popular Lectures and Addresses*, vol i
Thomson, William *Proceedings of the Royal Society of Edinburgh*, vol vi, pp. 94-105 (reprinted in *Phil. Mag.*, vol xxxiv, 1867, pp 15-24)
Vallee, Jacques *The Invisible College*, Dutton, New York, 1975, (published in Britain as *UFOs: The Psychic Solution*, Panther, 1977)
Wilhem, Richard (ed) *I Ching*, Routledge & Kegan Paul, 1951
Yogananda, Paramahansa *Autobiography of a Yogi*, Rider, 1987

For permission to quote extracts we would like to thank the following:

W. H. Allen & Co plc, for *The Prince and the Paranormal*

American Society for Psychical Research Inc, for *Appearance and Disappearance of Objects in the Presence of Sri Sathya Sai Baba*

Chatto & Windus Ltd and Mrs Laura Huxley, for *The Doors of Perception*

Collins Publishers, for *Chance and Necessity*

The C.W.Daniel Company Ltd, 1 Church Path, Saffron Walden, Essex CB10 1JP, England, for *Blueprint for Immortality* and *Design for Destiny*

Doubleday, for *The Cosmic Connection*

The Findhorn Press and Harper & Row for *The Findhorn Garden*

Grafton Books, for *UFOs: The Psychic Solution*

Michael Joseph Ltd, for *The Intelligent Universe*

Frederick Lenz and Macmillan Publishing Co, New York, for *Lifetimes*. Excerpts reprinted with permission of Bobbs-Merrill, an imprint of Macmillan Publishing Co, copyright © 1979, Frederick Lenz.

Mockingbird Books Inc.,for *Life After Life*

The Random Century Group Ltd, for *A New Science of Life* and *Miracles are My Visiting Cards*

Penguin Books and Princeton University Press for *The I Ching or Book of Changes*, (Arkana, 1989), copyright © Bollingen Foundation Inc, 1950, 1967

Self-Realization Fellowship, for *Autobiography of a Yogi*, by Paramahansa Yogananda, copyright © 1946 by Paramahansa Yogananda, renewed 1974 by Self-Realisation Fellowship. Copyright © Self-Realisation Fellowship. All rights reserved. Reprinted with permission.

Sidgwick & Jackson, for *The UFO Phenomenon*

For supplying photographs we would like to thank:

Cold Spring Harbor Laboratory, for photographs of scale models of DNA, from *Cold Spring Harbor Symposia in Quantitative Biology*, Vol XLII, 1977

Mary Evans Picture Library, for Albert Einstein and Sir J J Thomson

The Findhorn Foundation, for Peter and Eileen Caddy, Dorothy Maclean and Roc

Fortean Picture Library, for Fatima, Garabandal and Zeitoun

Ann Ronan Picture Library, for the vortex smoke box, from *Science for All*, 1880

Photograph of William Thomson reproduced by kind permission of the President and Council of The Royal Society

Photograph of James Clerk Maxwell reproduced by courtesy of the Master and Fellows of Trinity College, Cambridge

Yale University Archives, Manuscripts & Archives, Yale University Library, for Professor Harold Saxton Burr

Index